# Lyrical
# Life Science
## Volume 3

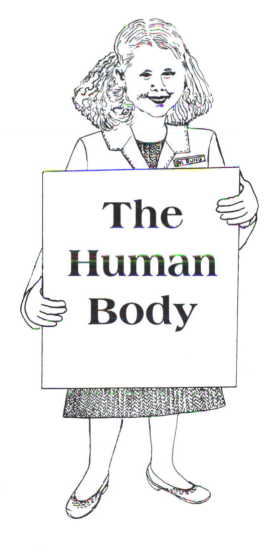

The
Human
Body

**Text and Lyrics
by
Dorry Eldon**

**Performed
by
Bobby Horton**

with assistance
from
Laura S. Rung, M.D.

Published by:
Lyrical Learning
8008 Cardwell Hill Dr.
Corvallis, OR 97330
541-754-3579

These book and CD sets can be used by students of many ages. Younger elementary students can benefit by becoming familiar with scientific terms through casual listening, yet may not fully understand the information until later. These songs, texts, and workbooks were written with middle school students in mind, as an introduction to life science. The information presented in these three volumes of life science should be very familiar to high school students before they study biology in greater depth.

Workbooks are also available for each volume. Ideally, these resources should be in addition to hands-on activities where observations and applications can be made. In this way the knowledge learned through singing and reading can also become known through experience.

Our website www.lyricallearning.com has reviews and awards; FAQs; an article about the theory and research behind using lyrics and music for learning; information about our products; and a list of our distributors and ordering information.

Text and lyrics: Dorry Eldon
Layout and design: Dorry Eldon
Cover art and design: Susan Moore
Illustrations: Eric Altendorf
Whimsical drawings: Sally Raskauskas
Sheet music layout: Bradley Ryan
Scientific advisor: Dr. Laura Rung
Editing: Roberta Sobotka, Doug Eldon, and Anne Hetherington

Printed in the USA

Lyrical Learning products include:
    Lyrical Life Science Volume 1: Bacteria to Birds
    Lyrical Life Science Volume 2: Mammals, Ecology, and Biomes
    Lyrical Life Science Volume 3: The Human Body
    Lyrical Earth Science: Geology

Volume 3 Text, CD and workbook set: ISBN 0-9646367-6-X

# TABLE OF CONTENTS

# INTRODUCTION

Welcome to *Lyrical Life Science Volume 3 The Human Body*. We hope you enjoy this musical adventure as you learn and comprehend how intricate and incredible your body really is. If you've taken your body for granted in the past, we hope as you sing along, you will gain a new awareness and appreciation of yourself.

Because the study of the human body is complicated, doctors and scientists long ago classified it into several systems that are distinct but connected. We have followed this example by dividing our study into eleven different systems so you can more easily understand all the parts that make up you.

Music has always formed the backbone of *Lyrical Life Science* text and cassette tape sets—*The Human Body* is no exception. But this time we have traveled beyond the United States in our musical wanderings. Delightful, well-loved, old-time tunes are found around the world and we have used several too good to miss. *Tarantella* is an old Italian standard most often heard now in television pizza commercials (these advertisers know a catchy tune when they hear one). *La Cucaracha* ("The Cockroach" in Spanish) is a nonsense song from Mexico. Who would think a song about a cockroach smoking a cigar would become a standard for generations? Ireland's lovely, mystical waltz, *Star of the County Down* forms the background for the study of the reproductive system; and the Caribbean *Jamaica Farewell* wraps up the study of *The Human Body* as well as the *Lyrical Life Science* series. We do hope you enjoy these faraway melodies along with some of America's favorite cowboy tunes, military marches and old folk songs.

Special thanks to our good friend, Laura S. Rung, M.D. for sharing her professional, medical knowledge. And another big thank you to Bobby Horton who once again put his heart, along with his talent and musical genius, into these songs to help children learn valuable scientific information. With all this said, get ready to study the human body in a way you never have before!

# LIST OF SCIENTIFIC ILLUSTRATIONS

# INTRODUCTION TO THE HUMAN BODY

(to the tune of "The Rebel Soldier")
The melody comes from an old Civil War song about a
lonely Confederate soldier far from home.

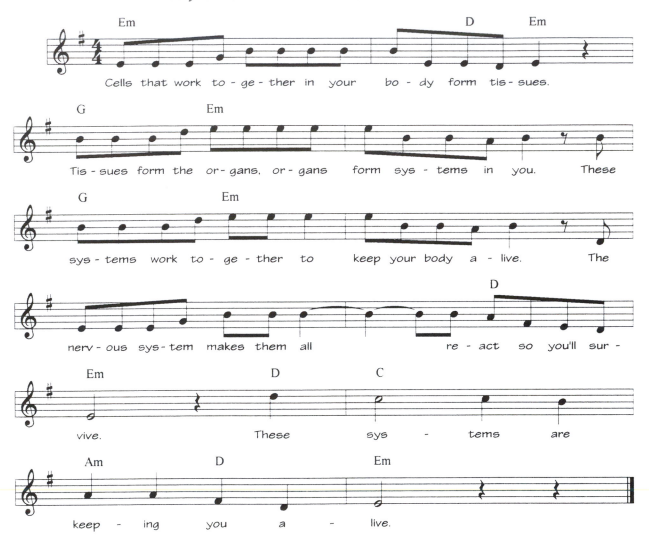

Cells that work to-ge-ther in your bo-dy form tis-sues.

Tis-sues form the or-gans, or-gans form sys-tems in you. These

sys-tems work to-ge-ther to keep your body a-live. The

nerv-ous sys-tem makes them all re-act so you'll sur-

vive. These sys-tems are

keep-ing you a-live.

Respiratory system uses oxygen you breathe
In circulatory blood is pumping by heart beat
Some waste is excreted through the urinary tract
Hormones come from endocrine and immune will attack
These systems are keeping you alive

Our bodies they are different for reproductive means
Digest for food absorption but we eat too much it seems
The skeletal connects the bones by the ligaments
The muscular like levers all control the bone movements
These systems are keeping you alive

# INTRODUCTION TO THE HUMAN BODY

Your body is amazing in its complexity of structures, functions and processes—all of which you probably don't even think about—that is, until you get sick or injured. Through the ages people have marveled about the human body—sages of old have proclaimed "I am fearfully and wonderfully made." There are modern echoes of that proclamation in phrases such as: "The human body, an incredible machine; the human brain, the ultimate computer." However it is described, your body is a marvel indeed!

You have over a hundred kinds of cells which come in all shapes and sizes.

Chromosomes: for cell replication

Nucleus: the control center

Cell membrane: marks the boundary

Mitochondria: powerhouses of cells where oxygen is turned into energy.

The cell: life's building block.

Your marvelously complex body is like every other organism in that it is made up of **cells**, the universal building blocks of life. Although you started as just a single cell, you developed to about 100 trillion cells!

Each of your cells can be distinguished from those of other organisms. First, your cells can be identified as animal cells because they do not contain chlorophyll, as do plant cells. Next, your cells are distinguishable as human because they have exactly 46 of the thread-shaped structures called **chromosomes**. (If you had a different number, you'd be some other kind of organism. Goldfish, for example have 104; dogs have 78—the same as chickens; horses have 64, gorillas have 48; kangaroos have 16; fruit flies have 8 and a species of ant has only 1.)

In addition to your cells having the number and kind of chromosomes for your "humanness," you are uniquely you because of the **genes** on the chromosomes. Genes make the particular patterns, or codes that determine your unique traits. They determine your hair and eye color, for example, and are passed down in your family, generation to generation.

Parents pass down their genes to their children.

Your personal 100 trillion cells can be categorized into 100 different types of cells. Cells that are similar join to make **tissues**. Tissues are groups of cells that work together to accomplish a particular function. There are several types of tissue, but these can be categorized into four main types:

**1-connective tissue**, as the name implies, connects, binds and supports your body parts. It comprises bones, ligaments that attach them and, surprisingly, blood cells. Connective tissue is the most common type.

**2-epithelial**, or **lining tissue**, covers your body on the outside and also lines internal organs, such as the stomach. It protects you from harmful germs but also carries out functions such as secreting hormones and digestive juices.

**3-muscle tissue** contracts so it can move other body parts, such as your skeleton. Your heart is one big muscle, but you have muscle tissue in your stomach, intestines and blood vessels, too.

**4-nerve tissue** carries messages as electrical impulses from your senses to your brain and then to every part of your body. Nerve cells make up your brain, spinal cord and nerves.

Tissues join with other types of tissues to make **organs**. The heart is a good example: it is made not only of muscle tissue which contracts, but also of nerve tissue to receive messages from the brain, and connective tissue to hold it all together.

Several organs work together in **organ systems**. For example, the digestive system includes organs united for the purpose of digesting food: the esophagus, stomach, and small and large intestine. Your body includes anywhere from nine to twelve organ systems, depending on the way they are grouped. They include:

| | |
|---|---|
| **1-Skeletal** | **7-Reproductive** |
| **2-Muscular** | **8-Immune** |
| **3-Circulatory** | **9-Lymph** |
| **4-Respiratory** | **10-Digestive** |
| **5-Nervous** | **11-Excretory** |
| **6-Endocrine** | **12-Sensory** |

These twelve systems interact and depend upon each other to keep you alive. What is truly remarkable is how the human body, with all its cells, tissues, organs and organ systems, works so efficiently to carry on all of the processes of life: moving, growing, responding to stimuli and reproducing.

Cells form
   tissues
Tissues form
   organs
Organs form
   organ systems
Organ systems form
   an organism

Four major fluids:
  1-blood
  2-lymph
  3-tissue
  4-intracellular fluid
   (fluid inside cells)

**All systems are lassoed into one body.**

Respiratory system brings in oxygen and gets rid of carbon dioxide.

Nervous system receives and sends messages and controls the rest of the body.

Immune system protects against invaders.

Muscular system moves the body.

Reproductive system creates new life.

Lymph system bathes the tissues.

Skeletal system supports the body and holds it upright.

Circulatory system carries food and oxygen to cells.

Excretory system gets rid of cell waste.

Endocrine system releases hormones into the bloodstream.

Sensory system gathers information about the world and relays it to the brain.

Digestive systems breaks down food into usable parts for cells.

# THE SKELETAL SYSTEM

(to the tune of "Tarantella")
"Tarantella" is a famous traditional Italian dance and melody, often
heard as a pirate theme song.

# THE SKELETAL SYSTEM

Simply stated, your skeleton is your body's framework that gives you shape and protects your internal organs. But your skeleton is not so simple—it's made up of 206 bones! Without it you'd be a shapeless blob. Insects and other invertebrates get their shape from "bones" that fit together like a jointed suit of armor outside their bodies—**exoskeletons**, or "outside skeletons"—which shed as they grow. But you wear your support on the inside, as an **endoskeleton**. Although you don't shed your skeleton, it does change as you grow. You have the most bones you'll ever have at birth: 350! But many fuse together until you have the 206 bones of an adult.

Birds have hollow bones to make them light for flight.

Compact bone

Bone marrow cavity

Cancellous or spongy bone

We usually think of bones as being very heavy, but many of your bones are somewhat hollow, not solid. All the bones of an adult weigh only about 20 pounds! This is an advantage because you need lightweight bones to move easily on land.

## BONE CONTENTS
Your lightweight bones are composed of 50 percent minerals such as calcium and phosphorous, which give bones their strength; 25 percent water; and 25 percent **collagen** (from a Greek word meaning "glue forming"), which cements minerals in the bones and gives them strength and flexibility.

Humans, like other land mammals, have lightweight bones so we can move easily on land.

Although bones vary in shape and size, they have these layers:

      **1-compact bone**: the hard outer surface of the bone, which also contains blood vessels and nerves in the Haversian canals.

      **2-cancellous** or **spongy bone**: the spongy, lacy network of bone in the middle layer.

      **3-bone marrow cavity**: the soft, innermost part of many bones, especially long bones, where red and white blood cells are made.

Stirrup, a bone in the middle ear, is the smallest bone in the body; shown enlarged and nearly actual size.

Manatees have solid, dense, heavy bones to help them sink to the ocean floor to get to their food.

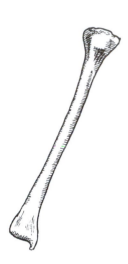

Long: tibia

In addition to bone layers, a thick membrane, the **periosteum** (Latin for "surrounding the bone") covers bones—except for the **cartilage** at the ends where the bones connect. Cartilage, as on the end of your nose, is flexible and can be pressed down or twisted but will return to its original shape.

### KINDS OF BONE
Your 206 bones are classified by their shape into four basic types:

> **1-long** are skinny, hollow bones such as the tibia and fibula in your leg, and humerus in your upper arm. The longest bone is the femur, or thighbone.
> **2-short** include the many bones in ankles, feet, and wrists.
> **3-flat** are bones such as the ribs, scapula, and sternum, or breastbone.
> **4-irregular** are bones of such diverse shape they don't fit in any other group. They include your vertebrae, pelvis, and the smallest bone, the stirrup, in your ear.

Osteocytes, originally from Greek words meaning "bone" and "cell," are the most common type of bone cells. **Matrix** is nonliving material between them, binding them together.

Short: index finger, the middle phalanx

Scientists classify bones into two distinct skeletal systems to help further the understanding of the human body. The study of the skeletal system becomes less complicated for all of us when we know that any bone, no matter what size or shape, is considered part of either the **axial** or **appendicular** skeleton. If a bone is part of the structure going down the center—the axis of your body, it is part of the axial skeleton. If a bone hangs, such as in the leg or arm—appendages, it is part of the appendicular, which means "hanging."

Flat: sternum

### AXIAL SKELETON
Bones going down the center of your body include:

> **1-cranium**: the skull
> **2-vertebrae**: the spine
> **3-ribs**
> **4-sternum**: the breastbone

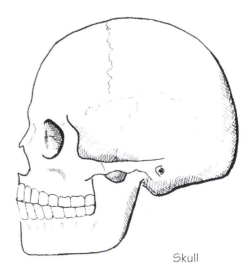

Women often put red rouge on their **zygomatic arches** (the cheekbones).

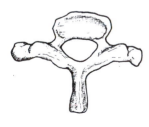

Irregular: vertebrae

### Cranium
The **cranium** is made up of 29 bones; it's really a bony helmet or brainbox to protect your brain. But it does have a few holes—for your nose, ears, and eyes. (So if anyone tries to insult you by asking if you have holes in your head, just proudly answer: "yes," because where would you be without them!)

Skull

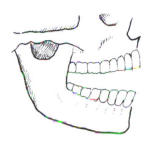

The bony palate is what separates the nose from the mouth. But your nasal passage goes all the way back to your vertebrae!

The only bone in your face that can move is your **mandible**, or lower jawbone. The mandible connects with the **maxilla**, or upper jawbone, at the temporomandibular joint (more about joints later in this chapter). Teeth grow out of these bones, and are necessary for all the talking and eating you do.

Sometimes people use their temporomandibular joints more than you'd like, as when they talk too much. To ask a friend for a little quiet in a scientific way you could say: "Would you please immobilize your temporomandibular joints?"

## Vertebrae: the Spine

The **spine**, also called the backbone, is made of vertebrae and keeps you propped up straight, like a post up the back of a scarecrow. But while your spine is stiff enough to support your body upright, it is also flexible enough to bend. The secret to this great flexibility lies in the spine's many small vertebrae (24 in an adult) and the discs that are sandwiched between each one. Each vertebrae is held to the next by **ligaments**, strong bands of connective tissue that hold bones in place.

Discs between vertebrae cushion the spine.

In addition to supporting you in an upright position, your spine protects your spinal cord, a major part of your nervous system that controls your body. Each vertebrae has a hole in it the size of a thumb, through which the spinal cord travels the length of your spine.

## Ribs and Sternum

Your **ribs** form a protective cage for your heart, lungs, and other internal organs. They connect in the back at your spine, wrap around the front, and attach by cartilage to your **sternum** or breastbone, a dagger-shaped bone at midchest. You have twelve pairs of ribs, but some of the lower ribs fuse with others and the lowest two are very short and hang free (your spare ribs?). With the ribs, the sternum creates your chest—it holds your priceless internal organs.

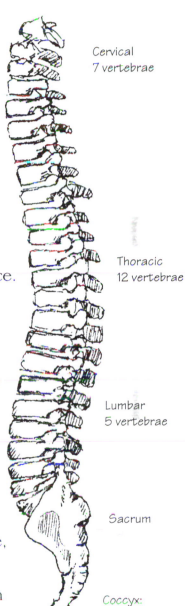

Regions of the spine

Cervical
7 vertebrae

Thoracic
12 vertebrae

Lumbar
5 vertebrae

Sacrum

Coccyx:
tailbone

Your personal treasure chest protects your internal treasure.

## APPENDICULAR SKELETON

As mentioned previously, the appendicular skeleton includes bones that hang down—that's simple and logical. However, the appendicular skeleton also includes heavy, crosswise bones called **girdles** that attach the appendages (legs and arms) to the axial skeleton. Girdles include the **clavicle**, next to the shoulder, from which your arms hang; and the **pelvis**, or hip bone, from which your legs hang.

### Shoulder

The **clavicle**, or collarbone, sticks out from your neck. Together the clavicle and **scapula,** the wing-shaped bones in the upper back, create your shoulder.

### Arms, Wrists, Hands, and Fingers

Next is your **brachium**—your arm. Brachium comes from the same word that means "arm" or "branch." (You'll find forms of this word throughout the study of biology. Brachiators, a group of animals that includes humans and primates, are able to support their weight with their arms: i.e., we can all swing through trees.) The upper arm bone is called the **humerus**. This is the funny bone, next to the nerve that tingles when you hit the end of your elbow.

Your **forearm**, or lower arm, has two bones. The **radius** and the **ulna** run side-by-side from the elbow to the wrist. Your radius is on the thumb side. At the wrist it is the larger and main bone of the two. If you have a radial saw, (a saw with a blade that spins) you can imagine what the radius bone does: it turns your hand. The ulna is on your little finger side. It is the smaller bone at the wrist, but becomes the larger and main bone at the elbow.

Your wrist is made of bones called **carpals**. Five **metacarpals** form the base for your palm. Four **phalanges**, or fingers, each have three bones. Thumbs, unique to the order of primates, have only two bones. But with them we can easily grasp tiny objects, a task that would otherwise be impossible. (Just try picking something up without using your thumbs!)

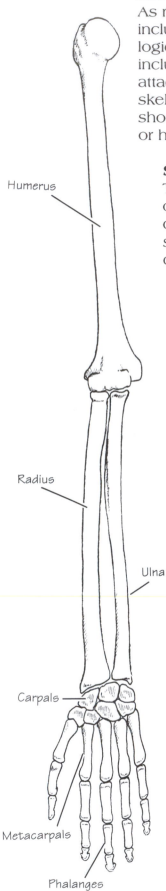

Humerus

Radius

Ulna

Carpals

Metacarpals

Phalanges

Clavicle

Scapula

Pelvis

### Pelvis

Your **pelvis**, or hipbone, is a group of six bones that form the **pelvic girdle**. It forms a bucket to hold your **viscera**—the scientific name for your guts, or intestines. The pelvis hangs off the **sacrum**, the last five vertebrae, which are actually fused together. The fused vertebrae and the mass of bone on each side look like a spear pointing down.

### Legs

Your **femur**, or thighbone, is your upper leg bone, the longest and heaviest bone in your body. At the joint between the upper and lower leg is the **patella**, the kneecap, which protects the muscles and joint of your knee.

Your lower leg includes the **fibula** and **tibia**. The fibula is the smaller of the two and is located on the outside, little-toe side of your leg. (Fibula means "little pin.") Your tibia is the shinbone you can feel in front of your leg; it's also what really hurts when you get kicked in the leg!

The fibula and tibia form an arch over the **tarsals**, the ankle bones, a collection of bones that create your ankle and heel. The ankle bones swivel, allowing your foot to flex. It's a complicated movement requiring a significant number of bones. Your ankles, heel, and feet contain a total of 52 bones, that's 25 percent of the total number of bones in your body!

**Metatarsals** are the long bones in your foot and correspond to the metacarpals in your palm. Your **phalanges** are your toes and share the name with your fingers. Like your thumb, your big toe is very important. When walking, you push off from the joints at the base of your big toe—maybe that's why it gets stubbed so easily when you go barefoot!

Femur

Patella

Fibula

Tibia

Tarsals

Metatarsals

Phalanges

## JOINTS

**Joints** are where bones meet—they give your skeleton the ability to bend. **Ligaments** (a Latin word that means "to tie") are strap-like bands that connect bones at the joints. Your body has three types of joints:

> **1-fibrous** are immovable joints (sutures), as in the bones of the skull.
>
> **2-cartilaginous** are slightly movable joints, such as those in the backbone.

**3-synovial** are the only freely movable joints. Between the bones at these joints is **synovial fluid**, a lubricant to protect the bones and make them move smoothly. Synovial joints include the following:

> **1-ball and socket** joints have rounded-end bones that fit into a cup-like depression—a design that allows many different types of movement, including rotation.
>> Examples: legs at hips and arms at shoulders.
>
> **2-gliding** joints have flat or slightly rounded bones that allow movement from side-to-side or back and forth.
>> Examples: some wrist and ankle joints.
>
> **3-pivotal** joints allow rotation.
>> Example: skull on the top vertebrae.
>
> **4-hinge** joints allow back and forth movement but no rotation.
>> Examples: elbow, knees and fingers.
>
> **5-saddle** joints have saddle-shaped bones that allow movement in several directions.
>> Example: base of the thumb.

> **joints:**
> where two bones connect
> **ligaments:**
> connect bone to bone at the joints
> **tendons:**
> connect bone to muscle

This simplified picture of the shoulder and arm shows how distinct joints work.

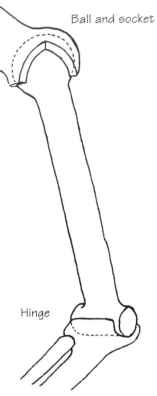

Ball and socket

Hinge

The elbow, a hinge joint, seems to bend like a bow (without an arrow). It bends like an "L" so it's an L-bow.

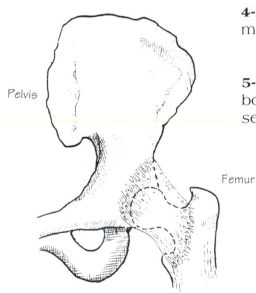

Pelvis

Femur

Hip joint: ball and socket

The joint at the knee is a hinge joint. But the reason a knee bends backward and not forward is because of ligaments. When the knee is bent the ligaments are loose; when the knee is straight the ligaments are tight and keep it from moving any farther.

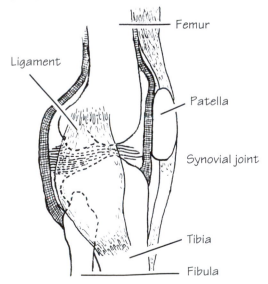

Femur

Ligament

Patella

Synovial joint

Tibia

Fibula

# THE SKELETAL SYSTEM

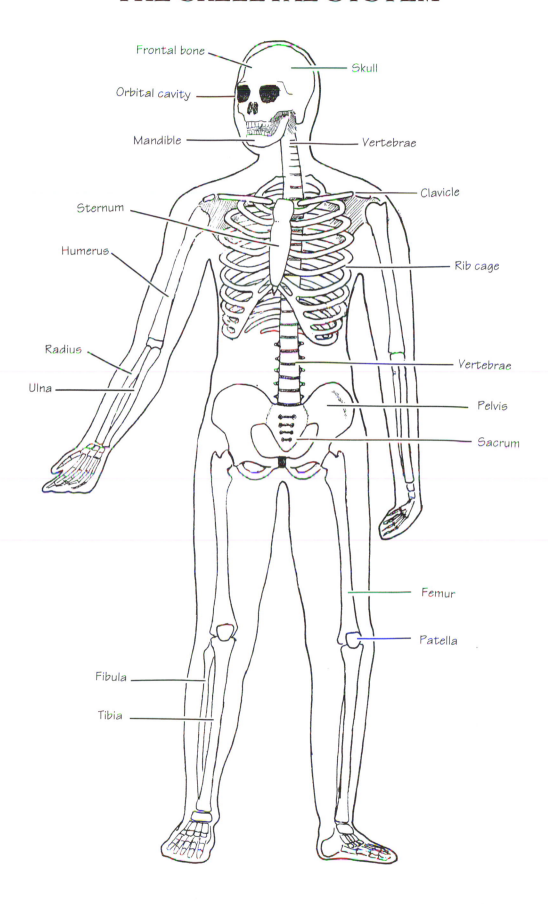

Frontal bone

Skull

Orbital cavity

Mandible

Vertebrae

Clavicle

Sternum

Humerus

Rib cage

Radius

Ulna

Vertebrae

Pelvis

Sacrum

Femur

Patella

Fibula

Tibia

# THE MUSCULAR SYSTEM

(to the tune of "Erie Canal")

"The Erie Canal" is an old work song from the early 19th century when men were digging the canal to connect the Hudson River and the Great Lakes.

Mus - cles of three types you'll find ske - le - tal, smooth, and the car - di - ac kind. Ske - le - tal mus - cles come in pairs with the bones you'll find them there. Work - ing to - ge - ther to make you strong. One gets short while the oth - er long. Like your arm when mus - cles flex bi - cep short and long tri - cep. Your heart is a mus - cle too. Ske - le - tal type work - ing like a smooth. A spe - cial - ized mus - cle called the car - di - ac, but your ske - le - tal mus - cles go right up your back.

Voluntary muscles all
Striated, the skeletal
Tendons at the bones connect
With the joints so they can flex

Involuntary are the kind
That move with no choice from your mind
Like your stomach with muscles smooth
And in the walls of blood vessels too
Chorus

# THE MUSCULAR SYSTEM

Your body is full of muscles —about half your body weight is muscle! You use your muscles for every move you make; they pull your bones every which way. They are the engines that make your body go; the forces that create movement. When these muscles work, they are in the process of getting shorter, or **contracting**.

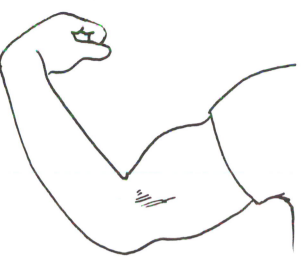

Your muscle contractions are controlled by **motor nerves** emanating from your spinal cord and brain. (See Chapter 4, "The Nervous System.") The end of the motor nerve that connects to a muscle cell is called a **motor end plate**. Nerve fibers fit into a hollow in the muscle cell; together the connecting muscle cell and nerve are called a **motor unit**. When the brain transmits an impulse, or message, for the muscle to contract, the nerve carries the message to the muscle cell, which in turn passes the message to adjoining cells.

To find your biceps, or "Popeye" muscle, make a muscle by bending your arm. The bulge you feel is the biceps. But if you didn't have the muscle under your arm, the triceps, you couldn't even straighten your arm! Muscle pairs such as the biceps and triceps are called **antagonists** because they work against each other.

As powerful as muscles are, these "workhorses" of your body start out just as your other body systems do—as tiny cells. Muscle cells are also called **muscle fibers** because they are long and somewhat stretched when compared to most other cells. The fibers join to form **fibrils**, which join to form **bundles**. Finally, many bundles combine to form a **muscle**, or **muscle group**.

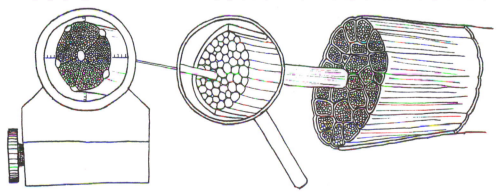

Fibers (muscle cells) make fibrils    Fibrils make bundles      Bundles make muscle or muscle group

Muscle construction

### KINDS OF MUSCLES

Muscles not only contract to create motion when you decide to do something like raising your arms or legs. They are also busy moving food through your stomach and blood through your vessels—when you aren't even thinking about them. That's because there are different kinds of muscles based on the functions they perform. All your 650 muscles can be classified into three different kinds:

　　**1-skeletal** move your bones.
　　**2-smooth** move your organs and vessels.
　　**3-cardiac** make your heart beat.

### SKELETAL

Your skeleton is covered with muscles so you can move your bones. These muscles are found in pairs working as teams because muscles can only pull as they contract—muscles don't push. To make your leg move you use a muscle to bend it and an opposing muscle to straighten it. Skeletal muscles pull bones into new positions.

*Forward march!*

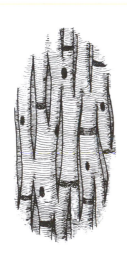

Skeletal muscle

You choose to move your skeletal muscles, so they are called **voluntary** muscles. They include the muscles that move your arms, legs, hands and even your tongue. In addition to the skeletal muscles being called voluntary, they are also called **striated** because the cells look striped or striated under a microscope.

Skeletal muscles are voluntary muscles. You choose to make them volunteer their services.

Smooth muscle

To help classify particular muscles, skeletal muscles are divided into the same two groups as the bones:

　　**1-axial** includes those that go down the center, or axis, of the body. They include the neck, head and trunk muscles.
　　**2-appendicular** includes muscles for the appendages; such as the arms and legs.

### Scientific names

Some muscles have scientific names that identify their location in the body, such as the brachii found in the arms (*brachii* means "arm"). Other muscles are named for their shape or size. The deltoid muscle is a triangle-shaped muscle in your shoulder named after the triangle-shaped Greek letter *delta*. Muscles may also be named for their characteristics: *maximus*—largest, *minimus*—smallest, *longus*—long.

Cardiac muscle

650 muscles　　650 muscles

Body builders exercise by lifting weights to make their skeletal muscles larger. They don't grow new muscles but make the ones they have thicker.

### Muscle fibers

Skeletal muscles are made up of two different kinds of fibers: **fast-twitch** and **slow-twitch**. Fast-twitch are the larger cells which contract quickly to allow for short bursts of energy. Slow-twitch fibers contract slowly and steadily. Studies have shown that sprinters have a high percentage of fast-twitch fibers in leg muscles, allowing them to run short distances quickly. Long-distance runners, on the other hand, have more slow-twitch fibers, allowing them to run distances that require great endurance.

In some animals, such as turkeys, fast-twitch and slow-twitch fibers are in separate muscles. The slow-twitch muscles are the dark meat and fast-twitch muscles are the white meat.

### SMOOTH

Smooth muscles are **involuntary** because they are controlled directly by your brain. There's no choice here—they *have* to work because the messages from the brain tell them to. You are not usually aware of smooth muscle activities, but sometimes they really get your attention with stomach contractions (hunger pangs) and intestinal cramps.

The cells of these muscles are smooth and narrow and perform tasks such as moving food through your stomach and intestines and moving blood through your veins and arteries. Smooth muscles are also part of the urinary tract, where they move urine through the kidneys to the ureter, then into the bladder, then through the urethra.

You may not often think of your smooth muscles, but you really notice them when you have stomach or intestinal cramps!

### CARDIAC

Cardiac muscle cells make up your heart (cardiac means "heart"). This muscle is so strong that it keeps contracting throughout your life—100,000 beats per day! The cells are a combination of characteristics of the other two types of muscle. Although they look striated, their rhythmic contractions are those of the smooth, involuntary muscle.

### MUSCLES AND EXERCISE

After muscle cells contract they need to have some recovery time before they contract again. During exercise, they build up **lactic acid** and **carbon dioxide** as waste. These make their job more difficult, and the muscle becomes **fatigued** as oxygen is used up in the cells. During rest and recovery time the cells "breathe": they take in oxygen carried by blood cells, and give off carbon dioxide and heat. This means that after a long run, hike or some other kind of workout, your muscles will just get tired. Give them a little rest and they'll be able to do their job again.

Muscles need to be used. If they are not exercised, they **atrophy**, which means they waste away. This happens when people cannot use their muscles because of a disease such as polio; injury from nerve damage (causing paralysis); inactivity from broken bones; or other muscular problems such as muscular dystrophy, a group of diseases involving abnormal muscle tissue.

### TENDONS

Tendons are strong bands of **collagen** (made of protein) that connect muscles to bones and joints. For movement, muscles first pull on the tendons, then tendons pull on the bone. Your tendons are very strong—the attached bone will sometimes break before a tendon will tear!

Tendons are at both ends of your muscles. The muscle is fixed to the bone at its **origin** near the inner part of the body and the upper part of the limb; the other end, its **insertion**, is attached away from the center of the body towards the end of a limb. When the muscle contracts, the origin remains still while the insertion moves.

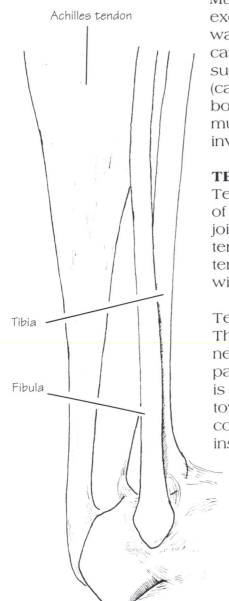

Achilles tendon

Tibia

Fibula

Calcaneus (heel bone)

The Achilles tendon is the strongest tendon you have. It attaches the gastrocnemius (your calf muscle) to your heel bone. The gastrocnemius is only one of 200 muscles you use for walking!

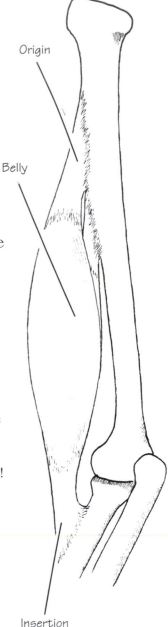

Origin

Belly

Insertion

The biceps muscle is shown. The **belly** is the rounded part of the muscle that "bunches up" when the muscle contracts. The **origin** is the part of the muscle attached to the bone that doesn't move. The **insertion** is the part of the muscle attached to the bone that moves.

# THE MUSCULAR SYSTEM

Back

Front

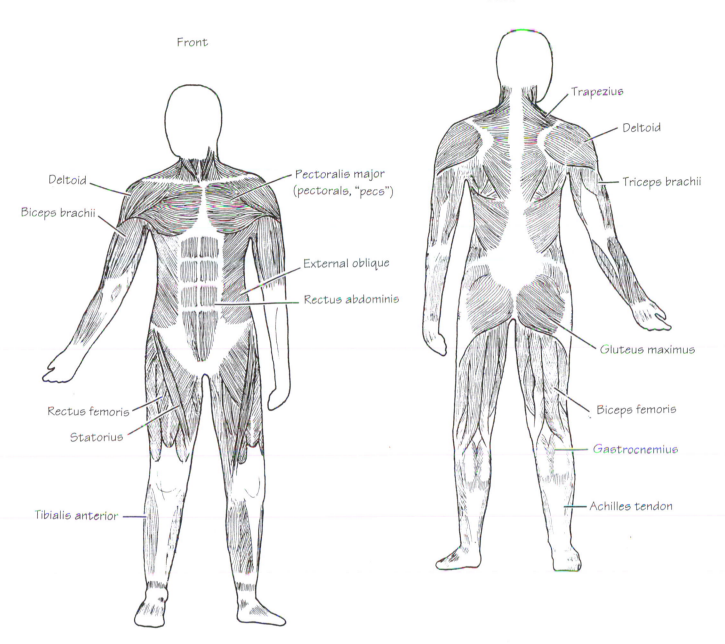

Deltoid

Biceps brachii

Pectoralis major
(pectorals, "pecs")

External oblique

Rectus abdominis

Rectus femoris

Statorius

Tibialis anterior

Trapezius

Deltoid

Triceps brachii

Gluteus maximus

Biceps femoris

Gastrocnemius

Achilles tendon

## Muscle Dictionary

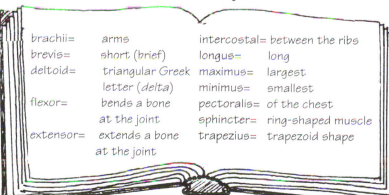

The small muscle that makes your top lip curl has the longest name: levator labii superioris alaeque nasi.

| | | | |
|---|---|---|---|
| brachii= | arms | intercostal= | between the ribs |
| brevis= | short (brief) | longus= | long |
| deltoid= | triangular Greek letter (delta) | maximus= | largest |
| | | minimus= | smallest |
| flexor= | bends a bone at the joint | pectoralis= | of the chest |
| | | sphincter= | ring-shaped muscle |
| extensor= | extends a bone at the joint | trapezius= | trapezoid shape |

Many muscles have long, complicated names, but if you break them down to their word meanings, the names will make more sense.

# THE NERVOUS SYSTEM

(To the tune of "Old Joe Clark")
Here's an old-time melody from the Appalachian Mountains.

Forebrain's hypothalamus and
thalamus and cerebrum
Hindbrain has medulla and
pons and cerebellum
Forebrain is for conscious thought
mid- and hind- make brain stem
With the nerves and spinal cord
for communication
Chorus

Fibers in the cells are the
dendrites and the axons
Covered with a myelin sheath
help the current pass on
Jumping gaps at the synapse
dendrite from the axon
With nucleus, cell bodies are
all part of your neuron
Chorus

Doesn't even use the brain
the system autonomic
Messages to innards are
Rather automatic
Changes when you're angry are
from the sympathetic
Changes when you're calming down
from parasympathetic
Chorus

# THE NERVOUS SYSTEM

Your nervous system is your body's communication system. It relays information from the senses, organs, glands, and muscles to the brain. Your brain decides the appropriate response and sends its message back—all in the wink of an eye! Billions and billions of specialized messenger cells, **nerve cells**, make up this system, which can do everything from a simple reflex action to deep intellectual reasoning. The nervous system—the message system—is made up of three parts:

> **1-brain**: the control center of your entire body makes up only 2 percent of your body weight.
> **2-spinal cord**: the long rope of nerves running the length of the spine connects the brain with the rest of the body.
> **3-nerves**: the long bundles of **nerve cells** emerging from the brain and spinal cord reach into all the muscles and organs.

The brain and spinal cord make up the **central nervous system**—it is so central to everything about you. The nerves make up the **peripheral nervous system**, reaching to your outer parts.

### NERVE CELLS

Before you were born your body was quickly producing thread-like nerve cells, also called **neurons**. At birth you had all the neurons you'll have for your whole life because, unlike other cells, they can't reproduce themselves. This creates real problems for people whose brain, spinal cord, or nerves have been damaged. Nerve cells have not only the structures found in other cells, such as a cell body and nucleus, but they also have two unique features collectively called **nerve fibers**:

> **1-dendrites**: little branches extending off the nerve cell body <u>receive</u> messages. *Dendrite* comes from a Greek word meaning "tree."
> **2-axon:** the longest branch off the cell body <u>passes</u> messages on to the next cell.

Dendrites and axons usually have a white covering around them called a **myelin sheath**. It works like insulation does around an electric wire, helping the nerve fibers to carry their messages faster and without interference.

---

**No Diving**

To protect your nervous system, especially your spinal cord, never dive into shallow water. A broken neck may sever the spinal cord, causing paralysis.

---

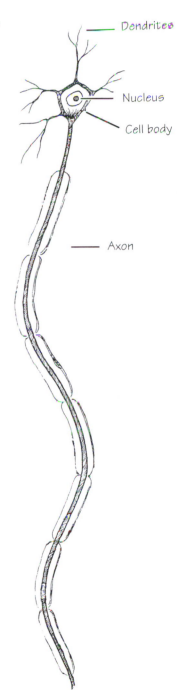

Nerve cell

— Dendrites

Nucleus

Cell body

— Axon

1-A **nerve cell** is also called a **neuron**.
2-The **cell body** is the main part of the neuron that holds the nucleus.
3-**Nerve fibers** are the dendrites and axons on a nerve cell.

A message comes to the nerve cell as an electrical current— a **nerve impulse** A dendrite receives it and passes it through the cell body to the axon. The axon passes it on to the next cell's dendrite but first the impulse has to jump a gap between cells called the **synapse**. The impulse passes through this space on chemicals called **neurotransmitters** released at the end of the axon. The process of sending the message cell-to-cell continues until it reaches its destination, which can be up to the brain, or out to anywhere in the body.

Cell body

Dendrite

Synapse

Nerve endings on the axon

Axon

*The nerve impulse jumps the synapse, the space between nerve fibers, as it passes from axon to dendrite.*

## BRAIN

Your brain sends, receives, and processes electrical messages from throughout your body. It coordinates, regulates, and directs every thing that is going on within you. It may look like a huge, three-pound (1.3 kg.) wrinkled walnut, but it is the center of your nervous system. That is why it is well protected in a brainbox: your skull, or cranium. Your brain is made up of 10 to 100 billion neurons plus many more **glial cells** (from a Greek word meaning "glue") to hold the tissue together.

*A bird's eye view of the brain showing the two cerebral hemispheres.*

The brain is surrounded by three membranes, collectively called **meninges**. They protect the brain and insulate it from shocks and knocks.

**1-** the outer **dura mater** is leathery.
**2-** the middle layer, the **arachnoid**, is spongy but delicate, like a spiderweb. (Arachnoid comes from the Greek word meaning "cob-web.")
**3-** the inner **pia mater** is a thin, soft membrane which follows the contours and wrinkles of the brain. (Pia means "tender.")

Under the protective meninges, there are three main parts to the brain:
**1-forebrain**: includes cerebrum, thalamus, hypothalamus and pituitary gland.
**2-midbrain**: connects the fore- and hindbrain and also makes up part of the brain stem.
**3-hindbrain**: includes the cerebellum, medulla oblongata and pons. The hindbrain and midbrain together make up the **brain stem**.

*Spinal meningitis is a disease which causes swelling and inflammation of the meninges.*

### Forebrain

The forebrain is regarded as the higher brain because it is most developed in the class of mammals. That class, of course, includes you, a *Homo sapiens* (Latin for "wise man"). Some of the major parts and their functions include:

**1-cerebrum** makes up 85 percent of the brain and is the thinking part. It controls conscious thought, personality, memory, voluntary actions, and reasoning. The outermost layer is the **cerebral cortex** (usually just called **cortex**). It's **gray matter** which consists of cell bodies of nerve cells. Like the inside of a walnut, the cerebrum is divided in two. The halves, called **cerebral hemispheres**, are joined together by a band of fibers called the **corpus callosum**.

**2-thalamus** transfers information from the senses to the cerebrum.

**3-hypothalamus** regulates body temperature, hunger, and thirst. It also controls the heart, stomach, intestines, and pituitary gland.

**4-pituitary gland** controls all the other glands of the endocrine system.

> **Gray matter** is formed by a concentration of nerve cell bodies. It looks brownish-gray and includes the periphery of the brain.
>
> **White matter** is formed by nerve fibers which project like tails from nerve cell bodies into the center of the brain. These nerve fibers are covered with white myelin sheath forming the white matter in the brain.

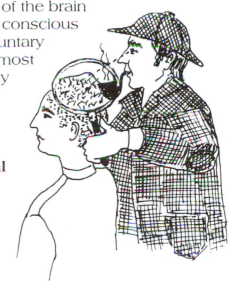

Phrenology was the study of head bumps. It has since been disproven, but even up until the Victorian era when the Sherlock Holmes stories were written, bumps were thought to reveal personalities. For example, criminals were thought to have certain kinds of head bumps.

Brain

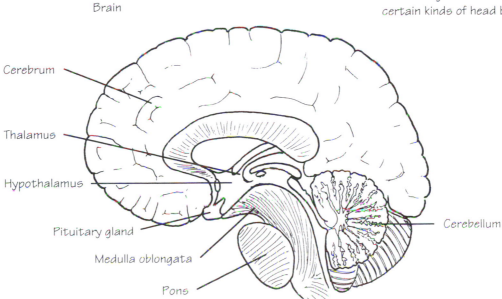

Cerebrum

Thalamus

Hypothalamus

Pituitary gland

Medulla oblongata

Pons

Cerebellum

### Midbrain and hindbrain

The midbrain is only about one-inch long. It takes in messages from the eyes, inner ear, and cerebrum and also helps coordinate movement and muscle activity. The midbrain and hindbrain are considered the primitive brain because all organisms have them—or at least those with a brain—from the worm to the bird. The midbrain and hindbrain make up the **brain stem**, which controls your body's automatic functions.

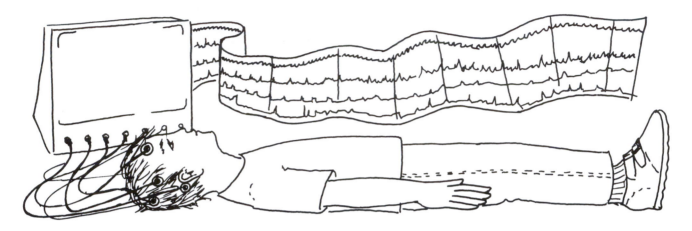

Brain waves are the electrical currents produced by the nerve cells in the brain. A machine called an electroencephalograph detects and records four distinct wavelengths: alpha, beta, delta and theta.

The hindbrain consists of three parts:

**1-cerebellum**: the largest part of the hindbrain coordinates your body's movement and balance. It looks like a small cerebrum—cerebellum means "little cerebrum."

**2-pons**: the link between the forebrain, the cerebellum, and the medulla oblongata in the lowest part of the brain stem.

**3-medulla oblongata**: the relay station between the brain and the rest of your body. It's your body's Grand Central Station—all messages pass through it on the way to and from your brain. It also controls involuntary functions such as heartbeat, blood pressure, and breathing.

### SPINAL CORD

Your body tissues, muscles, and organs send and receive messages to and from the brain by way of the spinal cord—an 18-inch long cable of nerve cells tunneling through the vertebrae in your spine. It's connected to the brain stem, and, like the brain, the spinal cord is wrapped in three layers of meninges for protection.

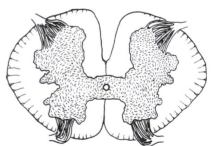

Spinal cord, a cross section. The butterfly shape illustrates **gray matter**, the cell bodies inside the spinal cord. **White matter**, the nerve fibers, are on the outside.

## NERVES

A nerve is composed of bundles of nerve cells and each nerve may contain more than a million nerve fibers! The long axons run the entire length of the nerve and can be as long as 30 to 40 inches (76–100 cm.). The peripheral nervous system is made up of 43 pairs of nerves, including:

**1-cranial nerves** (12 pairs): relay information to and from the sense organs, smooth and cardiac muscles, and glands. They branch off the brain stem.

**2-spinal nerves** (31 pairs): relay information to and from muscles, organs, and skin. They branch off the spinal cord between the vertebrae.

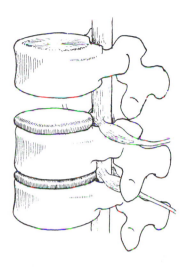

*Spinal nerves emerge from the spinal cord through gaps between vertebrae.*

When the spinal nerves emerge from the spinal cord, they branch into two distinct nerve types:

**1-sensory nerves** carry information <u>to</u> the brain and spinal cord.

**2-motor nerves** carry information <u>from</u> the brain and spinal cord.

The names of nerves emerging from the spinal cord often correspond to the major regions of the vertebrae. For example the **thoracic nerves** connect to the walls of the chest and abdomen; the **lumbar nerves** to the lower back, and abdomen; and the **sacral nerves** to the pelvis, legs and feet.

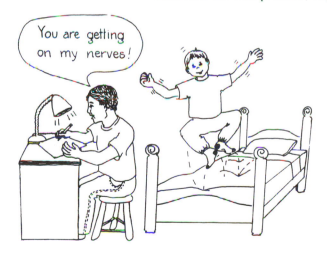

*Actually, irritability involves emotions in your brain—not the peripheral or cranial nerves.*

Your **autonomic nervous system**, part of your peripheral nervous system, carries messages to your internal organs. It really is automatic because you don't even think about it—it's unconscious and instinctive. It's made up of motor nerves to control your body's inner workings: blood circulation, breathing, elimination of wastes, and digestion.

A nerve impulse is sent from a nerve cell in the spinal cord to **ganglia**, clusters of nerve cell bodies throughout the peripheral nervous system. The message continues to other nerve cells until it arrives at a muscle, organ, or gland.

The autonomic nervous system contains two systems that work together, but are opposite in function:

> **1-sympathetic nervous system** prepares your body's reaction to pain, anger and fear. Your eye pupils may widen; your heart will beat faster.
>
> **2-parasympathetic nervous system** regulates your body for normal conditions. It calms things down after the sympathetic system gets them excited.

The spinal nerves are also divided into two different systems:

> **1-somatic** controls your voluntary muscles.
>
> **2-autonomic** controls the internal organs you can't choose to control.

Funny bone:
Most nerves are protected behind bone, but the ulnar nerve is more exposed at the elbow, so you feel it when it gets bumped!

**Reflexes** are another type of reaction you don't control. These reactions involve the spinal cord and nerves, but not the brain. Your body responds before you have time to even think about it. This shortcut is called a **reflex arc**. A sensory nerve carries a message to the spinal cord where a **connector nerve**—a nerve that connects sensory and motor nerves in the spinal cord—transfers the message to a motor nerve, which gives the message to your muscle.

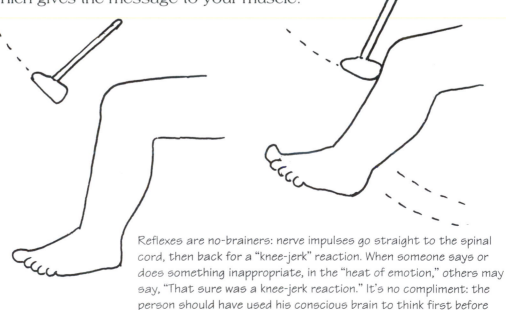

Reflexes are no-brainers: nerve impulses go straight to the spinal cord, then back for a "knee-jerk" reaction. When someone says or does something inappropriate, in the "heat of emotion," others may say, "That sure was a knee-jerk reaction." It's no compliment: the person should have used his conscious brain to think first before reacting!

# THE NERVOUS SYSTEM

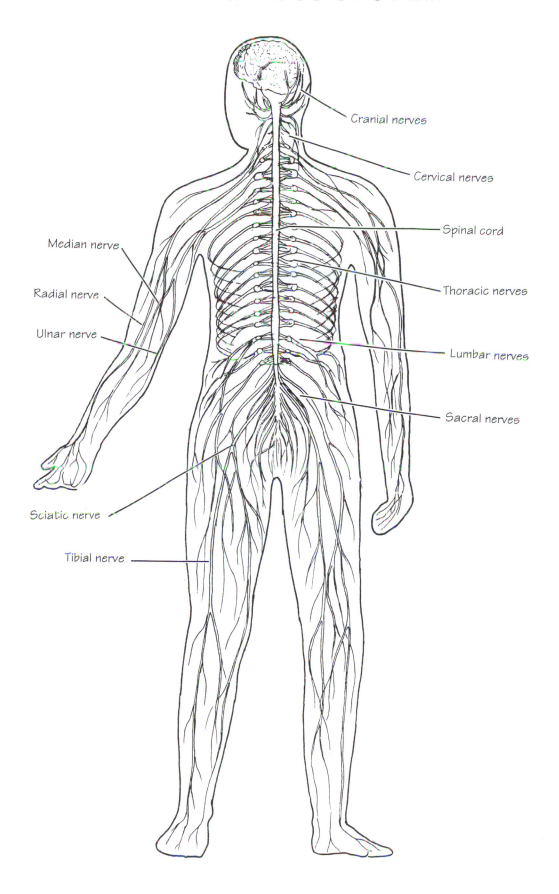

Cranial nerves

Cervical nerves

Spinal cord

Median nerve

Thoracic nerves

Radial nerve

Ulnar nerve

Lumbar nerves

Sacral nerves

Sciatic nerve

Tibial nerve

# THE SENSORY SYSTEM

(to the tune of "Caissons go Rolling Along")
The United States army theme song is a rousing melody.

Ear's di-vi-ded in three au-ri-cle the part you see, middle ear has three little bones. Coch-le-a's like a shell with se-mi-cir-cu-lar can-al in-ner ear so you hear all the tones. Or-gans spe-cial-ize to re-ceive the sti-mu-li to brain by nerves they take it in. Sen-ses num-ber five smell, taste, hearing, and your sight al-so touch with the nerves in your skin.

Taste buds for food you eat
Bitter, sour, salt or sweet
Papilla and with smell through your nose
With olfactory nerve
Smells the food your momma serves
Three conchae, sinus, and nasal fold

Chorus

Outer eye sclera
On the front it's cornea
Choroid middle of eye layers three
Ciliary to lens
Pupils to let the light in
Optic nerve, retina so you see

Chorus

# THE SENSORY SYSTEM

What you know about the world comes to you through your senses: sight, hearing, taste, smell and touch. Your five senses work closely with your nervous system. Your senses use **sensory receptors** to pick up and pass information to nerve cells, which pass on that information, now an electrical impulse, to the nerves. Nerves then carry the impulse to your brain—your senses are your brain's connection to the environment outside you.

### SIGHT

Your eyes are your windows to the outside world —you probably depend on them more than any of your other senses. The eyes, two tough balls filled with transparent jelly, have sensory receptors that receive information in the form of light rays. They take color images and send them to your **optic nerve**, which transforms them into impulses to send to your brain.

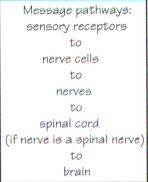

Message pathways:
sensory receptors
to
nerve cells
to
nerves
to
spinal cord
(if nerve is a spinal nerve)
to
brain

Your eyes are delicate, with inner-workings of several components arranged in three layers, including:

**1-sclera**: your outer eye is semi-rigid, giving the eye its shape. It's the white of your eye and in the front, the sclera becomes the **cornea**, the part you see through.

**2-choroid**: the middle layer of your eye is full of blood vessels, but in the front it becomes the **iris**, **ciliary body** and **lens**. The iris is the part of the eye with color, which is produced by a pigment called **melanin**. All eyes, no matter what color, have melanin, but brown eyes have more than blue. The ciliary body suspends the transparent lens and holds it with muscle fibers to help the lens focus light.

**3-retina**: the inner layer of the eye contains light-sensitive cells—the **rods** and **cones**— on the back inner wall of the retina. The rods, all 125 million of them, can detect only gray, but help you see at night. The cones, 7 million of them, can detect color and help you see during the day.

Tears flow from the lacrimal glands to wash and cleanse the eye of irritants.

### How your eyes work

Light rays enter your eye through the cornea, then through the **pupil**, the opening in the front of the eye.

Muscles in the iris allow the pupil to get bigger in the dark to let in more light, and to get smaller in bright light. The lens focuses the light as it passes to the retina where an image is formed by the rods and cones. The rods and cones "see" by firing an electric impulse when they perceive an image. These light-sensitive cells then send the message to the optic nerve which, in turn, sends it to the brain. The brain is able to make a picture out of electrical impulses!

Inside your eyeball you have a clear, jelly-like substance called the **vitreous humor,** which maintains the shape of the eye. Eyelids, eyelashes and eyebrows protect your eye.

Eye

Pupil

Cornea

Lens

Iris

Ciliary body

Vitreous humor

Choroid

Retina

Sclera

### HEARING

Your ears have two functions. One is to pick up sounds and transfer them as impulses to your brain; the other function is to maintain balance. The ear is studied in three parts: the outer ear, the middle ear and the inner ear.

Ossicles:

Malleus

The **outer ear** includes three parts:
> **1-auricle**: the funnel-shaped external ear gathers sounds and is the part of the ear that you can see.
> **2-auditory canal**: the tube leads into the ear and is lined with wax-producing glands to catch foreign particles and keep your ear clean.
> **3-tympanic membrane**: the eardrum forms a protective barrier between the outer and inner parts of the ear.

Incus

The **middle ear** is filled with air and contains the **ossicles,** your body's three smallest bones, which are named after their shapes.
> **1-malleus**: the hammer
> **2-incus**: the anvil
> **3-stapes**: the stirrup

Stapes

The **inner ear**, cushioned with fluid, is not only essential for hearing but also for balance. It contains:

**1-cochlea** is a snail-shaped, fluid-filled structure that converts sound into impulses. It works like a miniature piano but has approximately 20,000 "keys" instead of the piano's 88!

**2-organ of Corti** (in the cochlea) holds the "piano keys." It is made up of thousands of **hair cells** which vibrate in the fluid and connect with nerve cells.

**3-semicircular canal** forms three connecting arches that control balance.

The outer ear catches the sound; the middle and inner ears contain the actual hearing mechanisms.

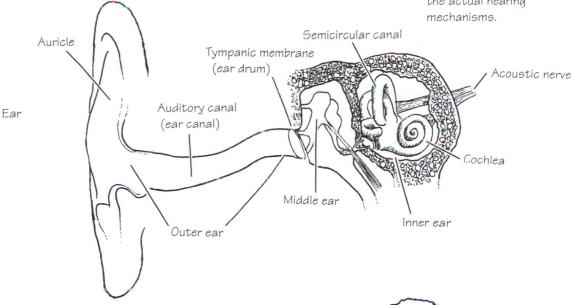

Ear

Auricle

Tympanic membrane (ear drum)

Semicircular canal

Acoustic nerve

Auditory canal (ear canal)

Cochlea

Middle ear

Inner ear

Outer ear

**How your ears work**
Sound waves vibrate the eardrum, which, in turn, pushes against the malleus, which pushes against the incus, which pushes against the stapes. These tiny bones transmit sound to the cochlea. As sound vibrations pass through the fluid, hair cells are moved, stimulating nerve cells to fire an impulse to the **acoustic nerve**, which sends the impulse to the brain.

Loud noises, including music, can seriously harm your ears, causing them to ring constantly when you get older. So, be sure to turn the music down.

### TASTE

Your sense of taste makes eating enjoyable! Imagine not being able to taste ice cream or your favorite pizza! To enjoy your food you have **taste receptors** located on **taste buds** covering the surface of your tongue, especially on projections called **papillae**. Taste receptors pick up taste as a chemical and carry it to nerve cells, which fire an impulse to nerves, which carry the impulse to the brain.

When you have a cold, you can't taste your food very well because you require two senses, taste *and* smell, to actually taste food. When you have a cold, the mucus thickens and doesn't allow the air-borne particles to reach the sensory receptors.

Different parts of your tongue contain different taste buds. You taste particular sensations at these locations: sweet at the tip, bitter at the back, salt on the sides, and sour on the sides toward the back. These four different tastes combine with aromas, which your nose senses, to create all the different flavors in the world!

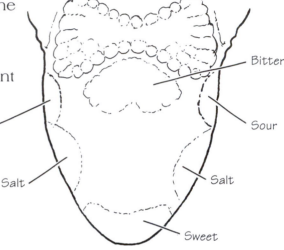

Tongue

Bitter

Sour

Sour

Salt

Salt

Sweet

Taste bud

Nerve cells

### SMELL

Closely connected to your sense of taste is your sense of smell. In fact, if you plug your nose when you eat, you won't be able to taste your food as well. We smell something when air-borne particles (molecules) of that thing, food, for example, dissolve in the mucus that coats the inside nasal cavity and touch the **olfactory cells** inside your upper nose. The olfactory cells are able to sense chemicals responsible for different odors, and when touched, will fire impulses to the **olfactory nerve,** which sends the impulses to the brain.

Three conchae: superior, middle, and inferior, are separated by the nasal fold.

Sinus        Conchae

Olfactory bulb; pathway to olfactory nerve

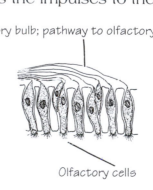

Olfactory cells

"...With olfactory nerve, smells the food your momma serves."

Olfactory cells, on the upper part of the nose, sense odors and send impulses to the olfactory bulb which sends them to the olfactory nerve.

**TOUCH**

Your skin serves several different functions and is therefore a part of different systems. In the excretory system it rids your body of waste through sweat glands while it controls your body temperature by giving off heat. It also plays a major role in keeping you healthy—it's the main barrier between you and the bacteria, fungi, protozoa, and viruses trying to enter your body.

Most household dust is really dried-up skin cells that have sloughed off!

Your skin is actually the largest organ in your body and makes up about 15 percent of your body weight. (So if you weigh 110 lbs., your skin weighs almost 17 lbs.) Your skin changes its characteristics depending on where it is on your body: it can be tough or delicate, thick or thin. The skin on the soles of your feet is very different from the skin of your eyelids.

Here's just a few things your skin does:
1-keep out invaders
2-cool down your body
3-get rid of waste
4-carry messages to the brain from the outside world
5-replenish itself

Your skin is also a part of the sensory system because the nerve cells in your skin give your brain messages about the things you touch. Some places, like your fingers, toes and lips have many nerve cells and are quite sensitive. Places such as your back, though, have relatively few nerve cells, and you may have a hard time identifying just what touches you there. But still, nerve cells are all over your body—even at the shaft of each hair, just waiting to pick up a message to send to your brain.

Skin has two main layers: the thick **dermis** is alive with nerve cells, muscle tissue, sweat glands, blood and lymph vessels, and hair follicles; and the thin **epidermis**, which is what is exposed. The epidermis has two layers; each contain **keratin**, a protein also found in fingernails and hair, and **melanin**, a skin pigment. The lower layer is full of new cells that push old and dead cells to the upper layer to be sloughed off, a process which takes about 45 to 75 days.

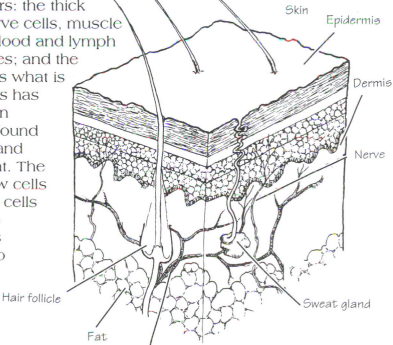

Skin
Epidermis
Dermis
Nerve
Hair follicle
Fat
Blood vessel
Sweat gland

# THE REPRODUCTIVE SYSTEM

(to the tune of "Star of the County Down")
This melody is an old, Irish waltz commonly played today in traditional music circles. The original, tender lyrics spoke of a man's love for his lady.

Verse: 1. Oh the male is a - ble to fer - til - ize the
2. In the fe - male's bo - dy the repro - ductive sys -
3. Egg un - niting with sperm's called fer - til - i - za -

egg in the fe - male's bo - dy with - in.
stem makes eggs in her ovaries with - in.
tion nurtured in mother's womb warm with - in.

When the male gives the seed to help cre - ate a
In her womb, called the uterus the egg be - gins a
Em - br - yo. then a fetus, and then a litt - le

life, then a new lit - tle babe can be - gin.
baby when this egg u - nites with a sperm.
babe is born nine months at full ges - ta - tion

Chorus:
For life is a mys - te - ry that we

live and our bo - dies pro - duce life to give.

Our genes and our dreams to the chil - dren yet un -

born to con - tin - ue life's cy - cle a - gain.

# THE REPRODUCTIVE SYSTEM

The reproductive system is unique compared to other body systems in that it is the only system you don't need for survival! Your other body systems work together, depending on each other to keep you alive. But the reproductive system doesn't keep you alive—it keeps the species alive and continues your family line.

Here's several pictures from the first *Lyrical Life Science* illustrating that all living things reproduce in one way or another.

All living things are able to make more of their own kind, to carry on their own species in the world. But reproduction is accomplished in a variety of ways; here are just a few examples:

Asexual reproduction: Mushroom—sporulation

**1-binary fission**: a single-cell parent divides into two copies of itself. Bacteria multiply this way.

**2-budding**: an organism produces buds to form new organisms which may break off, as with yeasts, or stay attached, as with large colonies of coral.

**3-sporulation**: an organism releases single-celled spores which mature into a copy of the original. Mushrooms reproduce by spreading spores.

Asexual reproduction: Coral—budding

These are all types of **asexual reproduction**, in which only one organism is required to make a copy of itself. More complicated organisms, such as humans, use **sexual reproduction** to create offspring. A child cannot be an exact copy because it has two parents. A child is a unique mix of the parents' characteristics, called **traits** which are determined by **genes**.

Genes are a chemical code, like a program, passed down from parent to child. They are banded together to make chromosomes, which are located in the nucleus of every cell in your body. The study of genes and how they are handed down is called **genetics**.

Asexual reproduction: Bacteria—binary fission

Every nucleus in every cell in your body has 46 chromosomes (23 matching pairs); every cell, that is, except your sex cells, which have only 23. It is thus possible for a sex cell's 23 chromosomes to pair up with

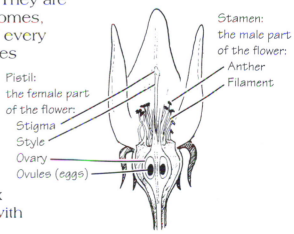

Pistil: the female part of the flower:
Stigma
Style
Ovary
Ovules (eggs)

Stamen: the male part of the flower:
Anther
Filament

Flowers reproduce sexually too.

another 23 from the opposite sex to make a new, unique person. The sex cell multiplies by a process called **meiosis** in which chromosomes are copied once, but the cell divides twice—creating more sex cells, each with only 23 chromosomes. These unique cells are made in your reproductive system.

### MALE REPRODUCTIVE SYSTEM

The male's reproductive system has the ability to:

> 1-make sex cells, called **sperm**.
> 2-place sperm in the female's body during **sexual intercourse**, also known as copulation, having sex, mating, or lovemaking.

*The male's sperm are the smallest cells in his body so this picture is obviously not drawn to scale!*

Head

Midpiece

Tail

Meiosis is sex cell division.

Sperm are created in two **testes** located in the protective **scrotal sac**, or **scrotum**. Inside the testes are 2,000 tubes called **seminiferous tubules** that make an average of 100 million sperm a day in an adult male! The tiny sperm travel up a tube called the **epididymis** to finish maturing, but even when they are fully mature, they are still the smallest cells in the whole body.

The mature sperm continue to move, now through a long tube, called the **vas deferens**, or sperm duct, and then through the **ejaculatory ducts** that flow through the **prostate gland**. During their travels in the male reproductive system, sperm mix with a milky fluid to form **semen**. During intercourse a man's **penis**, his external sex organ, stiffens and is inserted inside the woman to deposit sperm. Semen flows through the **urethra** in the man's penis and is released into the woman's vagina in a process called **ejaculation** (because it is forced out by muscular contractions).

### FEMALE REPRODUCTIVE SYSTEM

The female's reproductive system is more complicated than that of the male. It has the ability to:

> 1-make sex cells called eggs, or ova.
> 2-provide a safe, nourishing place for the unborn young to grow and develop.
> 3-give birth to the young.
> 4-provide food for the newborn young from the **mammary glands**, or breasts.

The female produces large sex cells called **eggs**, or **ova**, which are the only cells in her body that can be seen without a microscope. The eggs are produced in the **ovaries**, two almond-sized organs deep within the female's abdomen. Approximately once a month, during **ovulation**, an egg is released from one of the two ovaries and travels to the long, adjoining **fallo-**

*The female's eggs are the largest cells in her body. (This picture is also not drawn to scale.)*

pian tube (named after Gabriello Fallopio, the scientist who discovered it in the 1600s).

Zygote

The egg continues down the fallopian tube and is then released into the pear-shaped **uterus**, or **womb**, where a thick lining of blood has formed to protect the egg. If the egg is not fertilized, it will leave the body in a process called **menstruation**. Together, the lining and the egg flow out of the uterus at its base, the **cervix**, through the **vagina**, a long three-to six-inch (8–15 cm.) tube that leads out of the body. The monthly cycle of the thickening and shedding of the lining of the uterus is called the **menstrual cycle**.

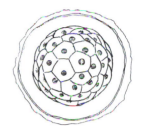

Blastocyst

## PREGNANCY

An area of study separate from the reproductive system is that of the actual creation of new life in the woman's body. Because you often see women with babies, it's easy to forget how incredible the process of reproduction is: our bodies—male and female together—can create new life! Even scientists find that the more they study reproduction, the more they marvel at its complexity.

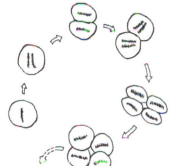

Mitosis is cell division.

Embryo

During intercourse, 300 million sperm are released to ensure that at least one reaches the egg. The sperm must swim up the vagina and through the cervix and uterus in search of a released egg. In order for an egg to be **fertilized**—the uniting of an egg with a sperm—the sperm must meet it in the fallopian tube before it descends to the uterus. If the egg is fertilized, it will then embed itself in the uterus lining, where it will grow for nine months. The uterus, the strongest muscle in the body, will expand many times its size as it cradles the growing new life.

Fetus

### Human Development

When the male sex cell fertilizes a female sex cell, the result is a single cell called a **zygote**. After fertilization and for the next nine months, the cell will multiply for growth and development through a process called **mitosis**. The 46 chromosomes in the zygote are copied before the cell divides, creating two new cells in the place of one.

About seven days after fertilization the zygote is called a **blastocyst**, a ball of cells. At this time it implants itself in the thick lining of the uterus. Once the blastocyst is embedded it is called an **embryo**. Even at this early stage some of the cells begin to develop into the **placenta**, which reaches into the mother to bring food and oxygen from her body. The embryo

**Ovulation:** the release of an egg from an ovary.

**Menstruation:** the monthly cycle in the female's reproductive system.

**Fertilization:** the uniting of egg and sperm, also called **conception**.

**Implantation:** the embedding of the blastocyst into the uterine lining.

**Gestation:** the growth of the zygote to embryo, to fetus, to newborn.

Newborn

From conception to birth the baby has grown from one cell to over six trillion cells!

is attached to its mother at the placenta by the **umbilical cord** and also is enclosed in an **amniotic sac** filled with **amniotic fluid** to protect and cushion it.

Only sixteen days after fertilization, cells have already begun to **differentiate**, an amazing but little understood process. Cells change into the different kinds of cells (skeletal, nerve, muscle, etc.) that make up all tissues, organs, and organ systems in the body. By its eighth week after fertilization, the embryo is called a **fetus**. Whereas an embryo looks something like a tadpole (!), the fetus begins to look like a little human.

Pregnancy is divided into three time periods of three months each, called **trimesters**. Each includes specific milestones of growth and development.

The **first trimester** includes the time from fertilization through 12 weeks. The tiny new human being experiences more complex development and faster growth than at any other time in its life. It grows from the size of a pin head to three inches (7 cm.) long. The different names reflect the tremendous changes that occur—from a single-celled zygote, to blastocyst, to embryo to fetus. By the end of the first trimester all of the external structures and internal organs are formed —down to the eyelids and fingertips! The heart even begins to beat at just 21 to 35 days after fertilization!

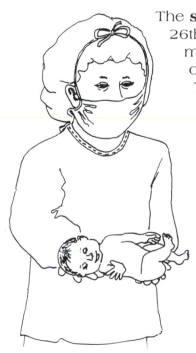

The **second trimester** includes the 13th through 26th weeks. The newly formed organ systems mature and the sex of the baby is now observable (through use of ultrasound). The next generation is also considered— all the eggs a female will have in her entire lifetime are developed now! Also during this time, the fetus moves and kicks with enough force and energy to be noticed by its mother. **Vernix**, a thick, white, ointment-like substance develops on the fetus' delicate skin to protect it in the amniotic fluid.

The **third trimester** includes the 27th through 40th weeks. The fetus continues to mature and prepares for life outside the womb. Fat deposits develop under the skin for nourishment and insulation, and lungs mature for breathing oxygen from the air after birth.

*"The best part of my medical training was the privilege of delivering a baby— what a miracle!" Laura S. Rung, M.D.*

# THE REPRODUCTIVE SYSTEM
# and
# FETUS IN MOTHER'S UTERUS

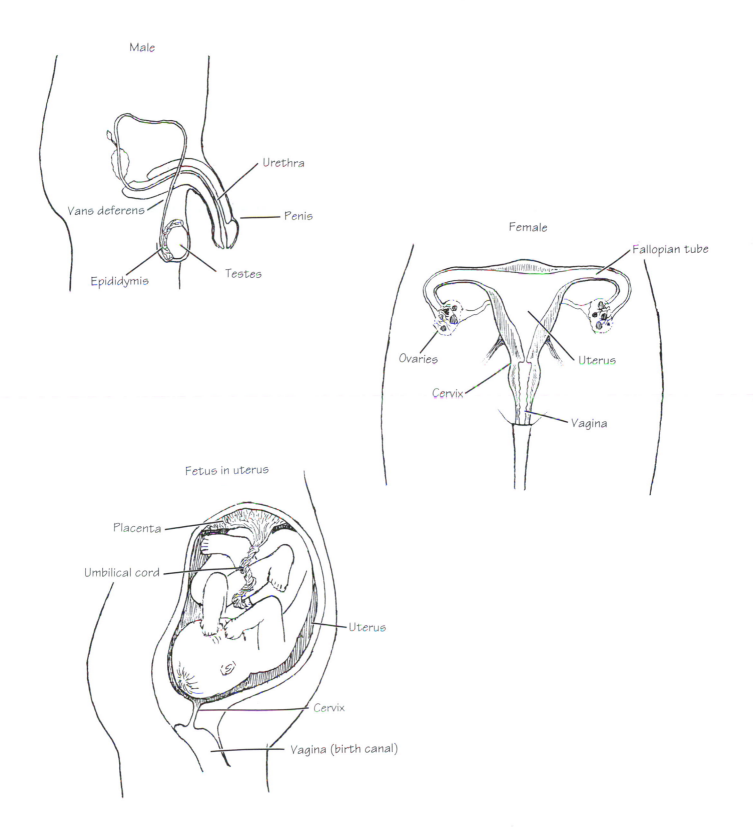

Male

Urethra

Vans deferens

Penis

Epididymis

Testes

Female

Fallopian tube

Ovaries

Uterus

Cervix

Vagina

Fetus in uterus

Placenta

Umbilical cord

Uterus

Cervix

Vagina (birth canal)

# THE DIGESTIVE SYSTEM

(to the tune of "The Coffee in the Army")
Here's a melody to an old song about the terrors of army food. Some
original verses you might hear at summer camp include gems such as:
"Oh, the coffee in the army they say is mighty fine,
It's good for cuts and bruises and tastes like iodine."
and
"Oh the biscuits in the army they say are mighty fine,
One fell off of the table and killed a friend of mine."

In your mouth there is sa-li-va it's
a di-ges-tive juice. It mix-es as your eat-ing with
par-ti-cles you chew. Then the food will tra-vel down a
nar-row tube called your e-so-pha-gus con-
tin-ues the pro-cess in the di-ges-tion of
food.

| | | |
|---|---|---|
| Oh, the stomach has a pear shape, the size of your two fists | And in the small intestine, there's pancreatic juice | And in the large intestine, there's feces as it's called |
| The walls are made of muscle creating, peristalsis | The liver makes the bile, intestine makes more juice | The waste then leaves your body, and now you've heard it all |
| There's pepsin, hydrochloric acid, too | For food to be absorbed and used as fuel | The four main parts for total digestion |
| Gastric juice makes the chyme | It passes through the villi | Mouth and small intestine |
| Within five hours' time | Cells it will satisfy | Stomach, large intestine |
| In the digestion of food | Cells need digestion of food | For the digestion of food |

# THE DIGESTIVE SYSTEM

The digestive system, also called the alimentary canal, is actually a 30-foot-long (6–9 m.) muscular tube reaching from your mouth to your anus. Most food you eat is unusable by your body's cells until you break it down, step by step, in a process called **digestion**. Digestion reduces food to its essential form so it can be absorbed by cells and be of use to your body.

## NUTRIENTS

Different types of food contain different types of components, or **nutrients**. Here are the seven main nutrients your body needs:

**1-carbohydrates** are broken down into simple sugars for energy.

**2-proteins** are for body growth and repair.

**3-fats** are stored for energy.

**4-vitamins** are needed for good health. For example, if you don't get enough vitamin D, you will have weak, brittle bones.

**5-minerals** are essential for body functions. In many areas of the world, iodine deficiency in children is still a health problem.

**6-fiber**, or **bulk**, consists of plant material that cannot be digested, but helps food pass more easily through the intestines.

**7-water** is often overlooked as a nutrient; however, your body is made up of 70 percent water. The digestive and excretory systems must have an ample amount of water to function correctly.

40% H₂O

Much of the water you ingest is in the food itself. For example, bread is 40% water; fruits and vegetables can be up to 98% water!

meal site

Plants make their own food, but animals, including ourselves need to eat other living things.

Digestion begins in your mouth. Actually, it really starts in your nervous system as your brain says, "feed me." The brain, of course, can't feed itself, but it can direct your muscles to move your skeleton to lift food to your mouth. Let's follow that food as it goes through the four parts of the digestive system:

1-the **mouth** begins the process of digestion.
2-the **stomach** is where most digestion takes place, but little is absorbed except sugar and alcohol.
3-the **small intestine** absorbs nutrients.
4-the **large intestine** reabsorbs water and holds waste until it is ready to be expelled.

To protect itself and facilitate food movement, the digestive system contains these layers:

1-**mucosa** is the wrinkled inner layer which secretes (pours out) mucus and **enzymes** (chemicals which cause the breakdown of food).
2-**submucosa** is a tough, elastic layer containing blood vessels and nerves.
3-**two layers of muscle** wrap around the submucosa to move the food along the tract.
3-**serosa** is the outer coating for lubrication as adjacent organs in the body cavity rub against one another.

## MOUTH

Food begins its long journey in your mouth, where your teeth cut, grind and pulverize food as your tongue pushes it around, forming it into a lump called a **bolus**. The first digestive juice, **saliva**, is secreted from three glands in the sides of your mouth and under your tongue. Saliva, important for "washing" your teeth and gums to keep them heathy, also contains the first enzyme, **ptyalin**, which begins the breakdown of carbohydrates, or starch. That is why, if you chew it long enough, a piece of bread will begin to taste sweet.

After the food has been thoroughly chewed and mixed with saliva into a bolus, it goes to the back of the mouth and down the **pharynx**, or throat. The **epiglottis** flaps down to cover your windpipe so that the bolus takes the right route, down the long **esophagus**, to the stomach. The food is moved along by wavelike contractions, **peristalsis**, from the squeezing of circular muscles located along the length of the digestive system.

The knife: another essential tool for digestion. Why?

Carnivores, meat-eaters such as dogs, don't need knives because they grow them in their mouth! Their carnassial teeth cut up their meat as they chew —but you need a knife because you don't have these type of teeth.

Your salivary glands manufacture about 6 cups of saliva a day! (Silverstein, Alvin, Virginia and Robert. *The Digestive System.* New York: Twenty-First Century Books, 1994.)

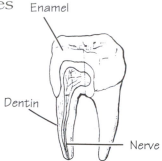

Enamel

Dentin

Nerve

The outside layer of the tooth is enamel, the hardest substance in the body.

**Deciduous** trees are those that lose their leaves. **Deciduous** teeth are baby, or milk, teeth that fall out before your permanent teeth appear.

Your stomach looks somewhat like the shape of a bagpipe's bag. Long ago they were made from an animal stomach, skin, or bladder. Today they are usually made of leather and covered with cloth.

## STOMACH

Your stomach is the main place for breaking down food into tiny particles for later absorption. Food slides into the stomach, at the **fundus**, the top part of the stomach where food is temporarily stored. The lower part of the stomach, the **pylorus**, churns and mixes food with **gastric juice**, a mixture of mucus, **hydrochloric acid**, and **pepsinogen** (which becomes the enzyme **pepsin** when it meets the acid). Hydrochloric acid softens the food and kills bacteria, and pepsin starts the breakdown of protein.

After three to five hours in the stomach, food becomes a thick, creamy, partially digested, semi-liquid called **chyme**. Simple sugars, drugs, and alcohol are absorbed directly into the blood stream from the stomach, but food particles are still not small enough to be absorbed. The chyme is then pumped (again by peristalsis) through the **pyloric sphincter**, a squirt at a time, into the small intestine.

## SMALL INTESTINE

Digestion is completed in the small intestine. After a long trip through the digestive tract, food is finally usable by your body. The small molecules can pass through the intestinal wall into the bloodstream. The small intestine is a 13- to 23-foot (4–7 m.) narrow tube containing three parts:

**1-duodenum**: a horseshoe-shaped tube ten inches (25 cm.) long.

**2-jejunum**: a nine-foot (2.7 m.) tube where digestion is finally completed and some nutrients are absorbed.

**3-ileum**: a ten-foot (3 m.) tube where most food is absorbed.

An average person living in a prosperous, industrialized country such as the United States will eat about 30 tons of food in a lifetime!! (Day, Trevor. *The Random House Book of 1001 Questions and Answers about The Human Body.* New York: Random House, 1994.)

The entry of food into the small intestine's duodenum stimulates organs to release more enzymes to complete the digestion process. **Bile**, a greenish liquid, is secreted by the **liver** and stored in the **gallbladder**. (Gall, like bile, is very bitter—so the name of the \holding tank for bile is perfect!) Bile breaks down fats to **fatty acids**.

Organs that secrete into the duodenum:
1-liver
2-gallbladder
3-pancreas
4-duodenum

The **pancreas** releases **pancreatic juice** consisting of at least four enzymes, to further break down food. Proteins are broken down into **amino acids**, their essential elements, by **trypsin** and **chymotrypsin**. Starch is turned into sugar, and then into glucose by the enzyme **amylase**; fat is processed by **lipase**.

The little pancreas is considered part of the digestive system and part of the endocrine system.

When food leaves the duodenum, it's ready for absorption in the jejunum and ileum. Millions of **villi**, tiny finger-like projections on the surface of the small intestine, increase the surface area of the small intestine. In each one are a network of capillaries and a **lacteal**, a vessel from the lymph system. Fat gets absorbed into the lacteal and goes directly into the lymph system. Sugar (glucose), vitamins, minerals, and amino acids get absorbed into the capillaries to be transported to the bloodstream and into the liver.

Food for thought about another kind of digestion: The purpose of this text is to make scientific information "digestible." This requires breaking down a large amount of information into its essential components to make it understandable.

The liver, the largest organ in your body, stores nutrients from digestion: glucose (in the starch form of glycogen) and amino acids. Then it can actually change the glycogen into glucose when you need quick energy and can rebuild amino acids into proteins for growth and repair. The liver is your body's chemical factory. It not only plays a major role in the digestive system, but also has 500 other functions including a major role in the circulatory system: it breaks down old red blood cells and reuses the iron.

Nutrients from digestion are put in storage until further use, but what about other food components such as minerals, water, and fiber?—They are absorbed or excreted by the large          intestine.

If the insides of the small intestine were laid flat, their surface area would be about equal to that of a tennis court. (Silverstein, Alvin, Virginia, and Robert. *The Digestive System.* New York: Twenty-First Century Books, 1994.)

### LARGE INTESTINE

Digestive waste, **feces**, is liquid when it arrives in the large intestine, then solidifies as water and minerals are absorbed in the **colon**, the first half of the large intestine. In the second half, the **rectum** stores waste until it is ready to be released through the **anus,** the opening in the buttocks. When feces are finally excreted, they contain about 30 percent dead bacteria, 30 percent fiber and the remainder consisting of dead cells and salts. Your body has used 95 percent of the food you ate, leaving only 5 percent to be excreted as solid waste.

Villi

The liver is a chemical powerhouse. Although the liver is a major component in digestion, it has over 500 other functions!

Large intestine

Anus

Small intestine

# THE DIGESTIVE SYSTEM

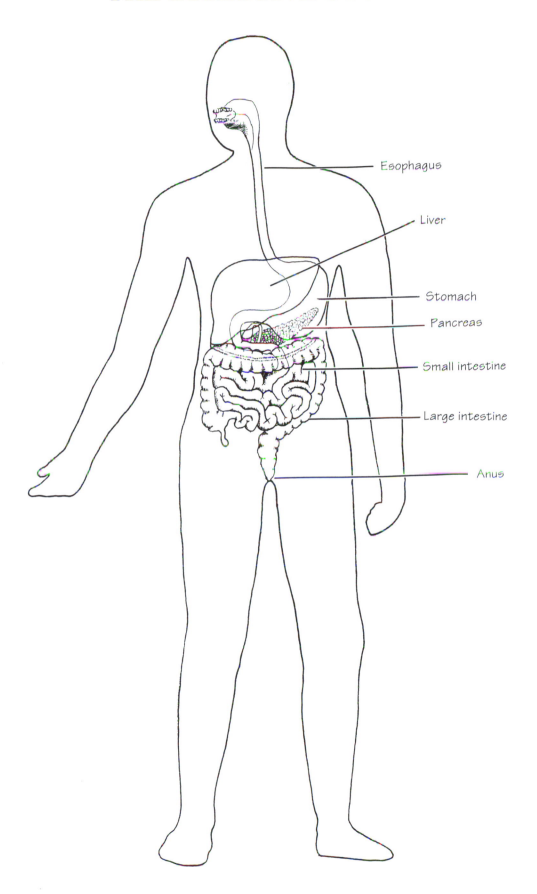

Esophagus

Liver

Stomach

Pancreas

Small intestine

Large intestine

Anus

# THE EXCRETORY SYSTEM

(to the tune of "Goober Peas")

This is an old melody from a light-hearted, humorous Civil War song about
a group of Southern soldiers eating goober peas (peanuts) in the midst
of the United States' bloodiest war.

# THE EXCRETORY SYSTEM

Your body insists on cleanliness and goes to great lengths to achieve it. Your body is designed to clean itself. Your excretory system removes cell waste from your body's trillion cells—keeping wastes and poisons from building up and crippling you.

Excretory system includes:
   1-urinary tract
   2-lungs
   3-skin
   4-intestines

Unlike the circulatory, digestive, and other body systems, many organs of the excretory system work separately; yet they all have the same goal of cleaning you from the inside out. Several organs of the excretory system are included in other body systems: lungs expel carbon dioxide; intestines expel bilirubin (hemoglobin from old blood cells); and skin excretes perspiration, ridding the body of heat and additional waste.

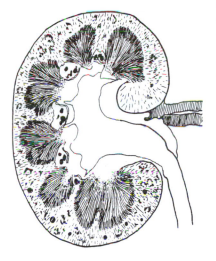

Although most people have two kidneys, it is not unusual for healthy people to have only one, or even four kidneys.

## URINARY TRACT

A major part of the excretory system not considered a part of another system is the urinary tract, or urinary system. The urinary system includes: two kidneys, two ureters, bladder and urethra.

Your **kidneys** are two bean-shaped organs about four inches long and three inches wide. They are next to your ribs in the middle part of your back. Their major job is to filter and cleanse your blood—in fact, every minute one-fourth of your blood flows from your circulatory system through your kidneys!

All this blood is purified by two million **nephrons**, the hard-working basic units of the kidneys. Each tiny, half-inch (1.2 cm.) nephron is made up of the **glomerulus**, the **Bowman's capsule** and the **collecting tubule** that twists and turns from it.

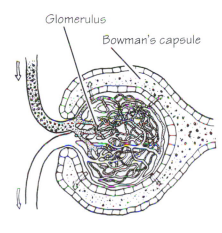

Glomerulus

Bowman's capsule

Bowman's capsule

Collecting tubule

Nephron
There are about one million nephrons in each kidney!

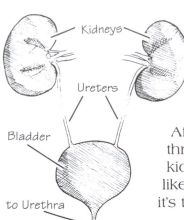

Kidneys

Ureters

Bladder

to Urethra

Urinary system

Nephrons reabsorb water and nutrients and take them back to the bloodstream. The filtered waste is **urine**. Urine contains **urea**, which consists of ammonia and carbon dioxide from the breakdown of proteins after digestion.

After urine is made in the kidneys, it travels through the **ureter**, a long transport tube from the kidneys, to the **bladder**. The bladder is the balloon-like sac that collects urine until the brain tells you it's time to release it.

## LUNGS

Although some carbon dioxide is excreted in urine and perspiration, most is given off in the respiratory system. Carbon dioxide passes out of the blood-stream to alveoli in the lungs, where you breathe it out.

## SKIN

You have two million sweat glands in your skin! Sweat glands are part of your excretory system even though skin, with all its nerve cells, is also part of the sensory system. Skin excretes a mixture of salts, urea and water in **perspiration**, which is really a dilute form of urine. Perspiration also rids your body of excess heat because your body cools as the liquid water turns to vapor.

## INTESTINES

Your intestines are part of the digestive system when they eliminate food waste. But they are also part of the excretory system when they excrete cell waste from old, broken-down blood cells. In the liver, red hemoglobin is changed into reddish brown bilirubin then excreted with bile into the intestines. There the bilirubin combines with food waste (hence the brown color of feces) and is eliminated.

During the Civil War, saltpeter, a by-product of urine, was used in making gunpowder for cannons and other armaments.

# THE EXCRETORY SYSTEM

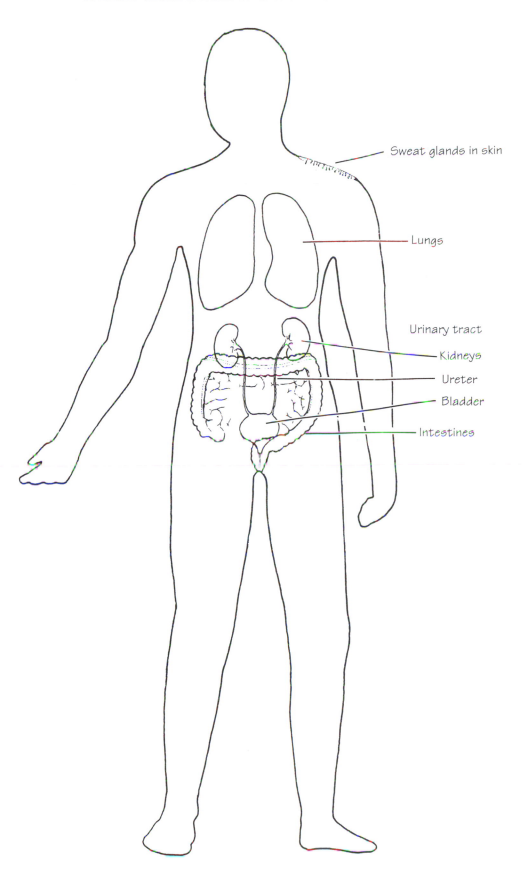

Sweat glands in skin

Lungs

Urinary tract

Kidneys

Ureter

Bladder

Intestines

# THE CIRCULATORY SYSTEM

(to the tune of "Red River Valley")
This tune is from an old cowboy song about a place and a girl in Texas.

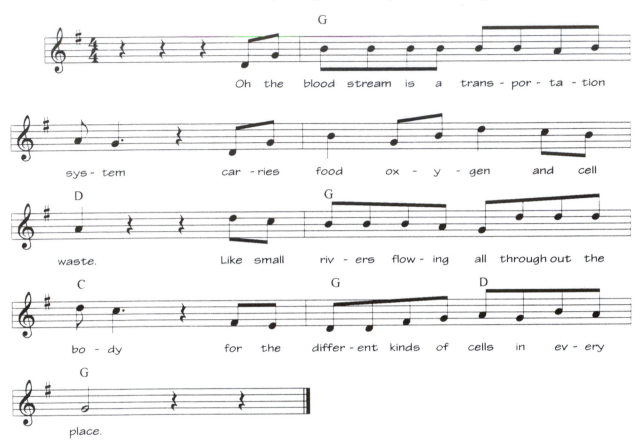

Oh the blood stream is a trans-por-ta-tion sys-tem car-ries food ox-y-gen and cell waste. Like small riv-ers flow-ing all through out the bo-dy for the differ-ent kinds of cells in ev-ery place.

Hemoglobin carries such precious cargo
It takes oxygen from lungs to the cells
Then it carries away carbon dioxide
And this waste at the lungs it expels

Oh, the heart keeps a beat to keep blood flowing
A---way from the heart in arteries
And the blood flows back to the heart in the veins
And they are connected by capillaries

Oh, the heart is made up of four chambers
The two large ones are called ventricles
At their top the valves are working like a trapdoor
Controlling flow from the two small auricles

Altogether it's the circulatory system
Pulmonary and systemic; there are two
Pulmonary to the lungs, it shortly travels
But systemic goes to all the parts of you

# THE CIRCULATORY SYSTEM

Your circulatory system is just what the song describes: a transportation system carrying food, oxygen and cell waste. You can think of it as rivers, streams and creeks all flowing within you. It is a perfect way for all your various cells, in all the tissues and organs, to get the food they need—and to get rid of their wastes.

The circulatory system is made up of your **heart**, the muscular pump that circulates blood throughout your entire body; **blood vessels**, the rivers within you; and **blood**, the substance which flows through them.

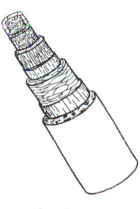

Arteries

Here's a little poem to help you remember that arteries carry blood away from the heart:
    Arteries: away
    Always start with "A."

### BLOOD VESSELS

Your blood vessels are tunnels of various sizes spreading throughout your body, reaching every cell in every tissue and organ. If connected end to end, your blood vessels would measure 60,000 miles long! Your body has three distinct types:

     **1-arteries** carry blood <u>from</u> the heart.
     **2-veins** carry blood <u>to</u> the heart.
     **3-capillaries** connect the arteries and veins.

**Arteries** carry blood filled with fresh oxygen—along with cell food (nutrients)—to cells. Arteries then divide into **arterioles** which become **capillaries**, tiny loading docks in organs and tissues where oxygen and food are delivered to cells. After unloading this cargo, capillaries pick up cells' wastes, such as carbon dioxide. The capillaries then drain into **venules**, which come together to make veins.

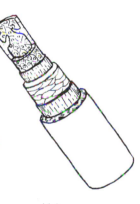

Veins

**Veins** carry blood filled with carbon dioxide to the heart, then to the lungs where you breathe the carbon dioxide out of your body. In this way your circulatory system works closely with your respiratory system: blood transports oxygen from your lungs and releases carbon dioxide to your lungs.

Arteries have thick muscular walls to withstand the high pressure of blood flowing straight from the heart. Veins have thinner walls with less muscle tissue because the blood flows back to the heart at a much

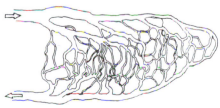

Network of capillaries joining arteries and veins.

Capillaries

(Not drawn to scale)

lower pressure. Capillaries have thin walls, sometimes only one cell thick, to allow chemicals to pass through easily.

The circulatory system is really two systems in one:

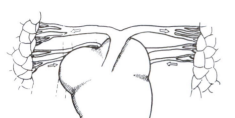

**1-pulmonary** carries blood to the lungs and back again. It's a short route using the right side of the heart.
**2-systemic** carries blood to and from all other parts of the body. It contains many miles of vessels and uses the left side of the heart.

The pulmonary system makes a short loop from the heart to the lungs, and back, not out to the rest of the body.

In the **pulmonary system**, blood flows from the right side of the heart to the lungs to get rid of carbon dioxide and pick up oxygen. Oxygen-filled (**oxygenated**) blood then returns to the left side of the heart, completing the pulmonary system's short loop.

In the **systemic system**, oxygen-filled blood leaves the left side of the heart to deliver oxygen throughout the entire body. The blood returns to the right side of the heart laden with carbon dioxide (**deoxygenated** blood). The blood then travels to the lungs in the pulmonary loop; then, once again, out to the body in the systemic loop.

**HEART**

The strongest muscle in your body is a hollow pump about the size of your fist: your heart. It weighs only ten ounces but it's strong enough to pump up to 5,000 gallons of blood through your body every day—and never quit your whole life. It actually is not one pump but two—for the pulmonary and systemic systems described above. The pulmonary is the one on the right that pumps blood full of carbon dioxide to the lungs. The systemic on the left pumps blood full of oxygen through the entire body. The heart itself is not too complicated to understand when you realize it's basically a pump made up of four chambers:

Can you imagine 5,000 one-gallon jugs of milk? Your heart pumps 5,000 gallons of blood through your body in just one day!

1) two **auricles**, or **atriums**
2) two **ventricles**

Valves in the heart and veins keep blood flowing in the right direction. They work like a trapdoor— blood can go in but not out.

On the right and left upper parts are the two small **auricles**, also called **atriums**, which are the receiving chambers for blood. The heart's pumping squeezes the blood through two one-way **valves** into large lower **ventricles**, the ejection chambers for sending out blood. Your heartbeat is the "lub-dub" of each valve closing as blood flows from auricles to ventricles.

**Other major heart parts**

The **pericardium** is the heart sac, a thin layer of tissue surrounding the heart. **Pericardial fluid** fills the space between the pericardium and the actual heart and works to lubricate the heart.

The largest veins in the body are the **venae cavae**—two vessels entering the right side of the heart; the **superior vena cava** flows into the top and the **inferior vena cava** into the bottom of the heart.

> Other terms to know:
> **Cardiovascular** refers to heart and blood vessels. **Cardiopulmonary** refers to heart and lungs.

The **aorta** is the largest artery, a whopping one inch in diameter, and is the main artery carrying blood away from the heart.

> The heart is a hollow, muscular organ that:
> 1) pumps fresh blood (blood with oxygen) through the arteries to all parts of the body.
> 2) pumps used blood (blood with carbon dioxide) through the veins back to the heart.

The arteries and veins in the pulmonary system switch the transporting functions that they have in the systemic system. The **pulmonary arteries** are the only arteries that carry carbon dioxide (instead of oxygen), and the **pulmonary veins** are the only veins that carry fresh oxygen (instead of carbon dioxide).

The **coronary arteries** rest on the surface of your heart and bring oxygen to your working heart muscle. All muscles need a blood supply with fresh oxygen—especially the heart itself because it is always working. Capillaries carry blood to individual cells and waste is removed by the **coronary veins**.

**Heart parts:**

Chambers
 —left auricle or atrium
 —right auricle or atrium
 —left ventricle
 —right ventricle

Valves
 —pulmonary valve
 —aortic valve
 —tricuspid valve
 —biscupid (mitral) valve

Septum—dividing wall
 between right and
 left chambers

**Just outside the heart:**
 —pericardium
 —pericardial fluid
 —coronary arteries
 —coronary veins

**Major vessels to/from heart:**
 —2 left pulmonary veins
 —2 right pulmonary veins
 —1 left pulmonary artery
 —1 right pulmonary artery
 —1 aorta
 —superior vena cava
 —inferior vena cava

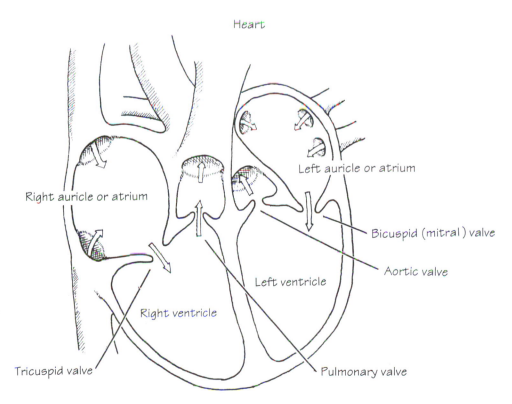

Heart

Right auricle or atrium

Left auricle or atrium

Bicuspid (mitral) valve

Aortic valve

Left ventricle

Right ventricle

Tricuspid valve

Pulmonary valve

### BLOOD

Blood is the substance that flows through your arteries and veins. It's reddest in the arteries when it's filled with oxygen, and bluest in the veins when it's filled with carbon dioxide. Depending on your size and age, you have anywhere from five to six quarts of blood. It has four major purposes:

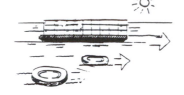

**1-transportation**: to carry oxygen, nutrients and waste.

**2-protection**: to clot up and make a natural bandage at a wound site. It also carries cells that will attack bacteria and invaders.

**3-communication**: to pass hormones, chemical messages from the endocrine glands, to various tissues and glands.

**4-temperature regulation**: to carry heat to the skin as it flows through the body. If you are cold, your blood vessels will constrict to keep blood away from the skin surface. If you are warm, your blood vessels will open more fully to allow more heat to reach the skin.

*Red blood cells are like barges, floating unpropelled in the bloodstream with their load of cargo.*

There are several components to blood, including small amounts of sugars, hormones, and nutrients; but **plasma**, the watery, fluid part of blood, makes up 55 percent. The other major components are three kinds of cells:

**1-red blood cells**
**2-platelets**
**3-white blood cells**

*White blood cells are like warships that search out and destroy invading enemies such as bacteria.*

The cargo ships in the system are **red blood cells**, the only cells in your body without a nucleus. These doughnut-shaped cells deliver oxygen to and carry waste from other cells. **Hemoglobin** is the red substance containing iron which gives red blood cells their color.

**Platelets** are plate-shaped red blood cell fragments which enable blood to clot as they stick together at a wound site. Platelets float along in the bloodstream until they come upon an injury, then stick to it, forming a plug. They are bridge-building materials that give messages to other molecules to create a lacy web of protection.

*Platelets are like ship wreckage ready to stick to a wound site.*

*Your body has only three kinds of blood cells, but each fulfills a unique role.*

**White blood cells** are larger than red blood cells, though not as numerous: for every white blood cell there are about 600 red. White cells fight disease. They swim through the bloodstream and can even leave it to enter tissues in their search for intruders—germs, bacteria and viruses.

> Blood can be classified into four types depending upon the kind of protein, or lack of it, on the surface of red blood cells.
> 1-Type A if A-protein is present.
> 2-Type B if B-protein is present.
> 3-Type AB if both A and B proteins are present.
> 4-Type O if neither A nor B proteins are present.

If you ever lose too much blood from injury or surgery, you will need more. You can get it in the form of **blood serum**, from which platelets have been removed.

# THE CIRCULATORY SYSTEM

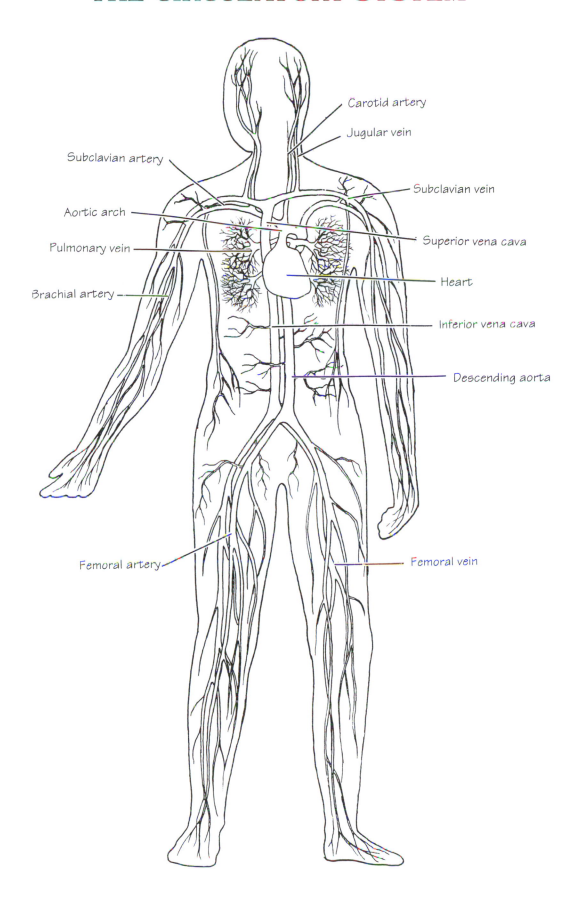

Carotid artery

Jugular vein

Subclavian artery

Subclavian vein

Aortic arch

Superior vena cava

Pulmonary vein

Heart

Brachial artery

Inferior vena cava

Descending aorta

Femoral artery

Femoral vein

# THE IMMUNE AND LYMPH SYSTEMS

(to the tune of "La Cucaracha")
The tune comes from a Mexican song about a cockroach
smoking a cigar.

Chorus:
Im - mune sys - tem with your lymph sys - tem
will your en - e - mies at - tack, with the white blood cells the leu - ko
cycte cells that will de - stroy and turn them back.

Verse 1. A germ is like a cu - ca - ra - cha that would love to live in -
2. Bac - te - ri - a or germs pest - er like with splinters when they

side ya. But white blood cells just won't al - low it
fest - er. Your bo - dy calls on the white blood cells

and when dis - co - vered will de - stroy it.
just to help you in those sick spells.

| | |
|---|---|
| There's several kinds of the white blood cells | The lymph is watery fluid |
| Phagocyte with macrophage cells | With white blood cells in a liquid |
| Their enemies they love to eat 'em | Bathing tissues, then as it flows |
| Wherever they hunt as they meet 'em. | Gets purified in all the lymph nodes |
| | |
| The lymphocytes include the T-cells | Lymph system is a sewer system |
| Messengers to all the B-cells | For all the tissues cause it cleans 'em |
| B-cells can make the antibodies | It moves the waste into lymph vessels |
| That match and remember germ armies | That move with no pump but with muscles |
| Chorus | Chorus |

# THE IMMUNE AND LYMPH SYSTEMS

Your body is almost constantly exposed to microscopic bacteria, viruses, fungi, and even protists, many of which are **pathogenic**, or disease-causing. Fortunately, your body has quite an effective defense system to protect itself. The first line of defense against harmful invaders is your skin which is usually a protective and effective barrier. But sometimes pathogens enter your body through cuts or injuries; or else enter through your nose, eyes, or mouth. When this happens, your body falls back on its internal defense, the **immune system**, which works closely with the **lymph** (or **lymphatic**) **system**—your body's cleansing system.

Both white and red blood cells are produced in the bone marrow.

## LYMPH SYSTEM
Your lymph system is another type of circulatory system, but this one has no blood and no heart pump! Instead, it includes a set of vessels streaming throughout your body, carrying **lymph**, a colorless fluid of water and white blood cells that bathe your tissues.

I clean my floors while lymph cleans my tissues.

The **immune system** is your body's defender. The **lymph system** is your body's cleanser. It also transports cells of the immune system.

### Lymph vessels, tissues and organs
This system doesn't need a pump because lymph flows through vessels by normal muscle movement. There are four main parts of the lymph system:

1-**Lymph vessels** include:
   A-**lymph capillaries**: the smallest vessels and the beginning of the lymph system.
   B-**lymphatics** or **lymph channels**: groups of lymph capillaries.
   C-**trunks**: groups of lymphatics.
   D-**ducts**: two groups of trunks: **thoracic duct** and **right lymphatic duct** drain into two large veins in the bloodstream.
   E-**lacteals**: vessels in the intestine that absorb fat when food is digested.
2-**Lymph nodes**: tissues in the paths of lymph vessels which:
   A-filter and cleanse lymph fluid.
   B-trap infectious germs and toxins.
   C-store white blood cells.

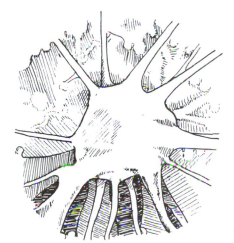

Lymph nodes filter out foreign particles and cleanse the lymph fluid as it passes through. Nodes, sometimes incorrectly called glands, are in nearly 100 different places, including the neck, armpits, and groin.

**3-Spleen**: a most important organ in the system. It is where white blood cells mature after their "birth" in the bone marrow. It is also where old, red blood cells get broken down and the components stored. Both blood and lymph pass through the spleen in their journeys throughout your body.

**4-Thymus**: located on your trachea; is another site where white blood cells mature.

Spleen

Lymph "leaks" from capillaries into nearby tissues. As it bathes the tissues, white blood cells hunt for foreign substances such as bacteria, fungi, or viruses. Lymph also removes "garbage" such as dead, damaged, or mutant cells, by carrying it back to lymph capillaries. The "dirty" lymph flows into capillaries and then into larger vessels which pass through lymph nodes where the "garbage" is filtered out, cleansing the lymph.

In essence, the lymph system is your body's sewer system. What would a city be without a sewer system?—A place of total filth! What would your cells and tissues be without the cleansing lymph system?—Awash in its own refuse!

Thymus

The white blood cells of the immune system can read surface structures on cells. This tells them if a cell belongs to you or if it is an **antigen**, an invader.

## IMMUNE SYSTEM
Most people are rarely sick, thanks to their personal, loyal army—their immune system. The name itself means "system of self" because it can distinguish cells that belong to you from cells or microscopic particles that want to do you harm. How? —with white blood cells, the essential element in the immune system. These amazing cells "read" chemical patterns on cell surfaces, identifying what belongs to you from what doesn't belong.

### Antigens
Antigens are surface patterns or structures on invading bacteria, viruses, and other germs which cause an attack response from the immune system. Here are just a few of the potential foreign invaders and the health problems they bring:

White blood cells swarm at an open cut to battle bacteria seeking entry. Pus contains the bodies of white blood cells that have died in the fight.

**1-bacteria**: cause tuberculosis, strep throat, and most food poisoning, including E. coli.

**2-fungi**: cause ringworm and athlete's foot.

**3-yeasts**: usually only cause infections in persons with weakened immune systems.

**4-protozoa**: cause malaria and dysentery.

**5-viruses**: cause influenza, measles, smallpox, colds, and AIDS.

### White blood cells

Your army of **white blood cells**, or **leukocytes** (*leuko-* means "white" and *cyto-* means "cell"), lives in every part of your body, but especially in your lymph and blood vessels. White blood cells can swim and even squeeze though capillary walls in their restless pursuit to search out and destroy germs. There are several kinds of white blood cells, each specialized to fight germs in a particular way. Two main groups include:

**1-phagocytes**
**2-lympocytes**

**Phagocytes** make up 60 percent of all white blood cells. They surround, engulf and digest, or "eat" germs—their name even means "cells that eat." This group includes small **neutrophils** and large **macrophages**. These cells will eat any unwanted particle or cell. Phagocytes are also involved in your body's **inflammatory response** to an injury or invasion, such as a cut or splinter. Bacteria enter the wound site, causing the surrounding cells to give off a chemical called **histamine**. In response, nearby blood vessels expand to allow more blood to the area—and more phagocytes to attack. The result can be painful swelling, but that's a sign your body is at work protecting you.

**Lymphocytes**, another type of white blood cell, can recognize and remember specific bacteria and viruses. Lymphocytes make up about 30 percent of all white blood cells. They are the special attack force of the immune system because they choose specific antigens as targets.

The **B-cells**, or B-lymphocytes ("B" because they are formed in bones), wait in the lymph nodes and, when alarmed, become **plasma cells** which make chemicals called **antibodies**. Antibodies attack antigens because they recognize the surface structures on the invading germs' cell walls. Antibodies neutralize antigens by producing a matching surface structure that fits into them like a key in a lock. This matching action also causes antigens to clump together, slowing them down and allowing phagocytes to easily catch and eat them.

Other B-cells remember the invader's surface pattern and will attack it faster should it try to invade again. This "memory" is what makes your body **immune** to the antigen.

Inflammatory response

1- bacteria enter wound

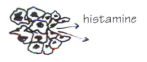

2- cells release histamine

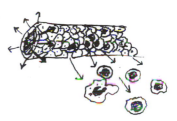

3- local blood vessel expand, phagocytes leave blood vessel to fight bacteria at wound.

4- wound area swells as phogaocytes fight bacteria.

**T-cells**, or T-lymphocytes ("T" because they mature in the thymus gland), include "scout," or messenger cells. As these cells float in the bloodstream, they check the surface structure of each cell they meet. There's no problem if the surface structure is acceptable as when a soldier gives the secret password. But if it has the wrong surface structure, the T-cells spread a warning to nearby phagocytes to come and get it.

T-cells also quickly move to the nearest lymph node to relay the germ's surface pattern to B-cells. The **T-helper cells** stimulate the B-cells to change into plasma cells and make antibodies. When the fight is over, **T-suppressor cells** stop the antibody production.

*Different kinds of white blood cells vary in their nucleus size and structure. Some look grainy while others look large and solid.*

T-cells also control another type of lymphocyte called **NK-cells** (**natural killer lymphocytes**, also called **killer cells**). These cells can detect and attack invaders such as viruses, even when they are hiding inside an otherwise normal cell. NKs rush to the virus cells and spew out poisonous chemicals that destroy them.

Soldiers re-enact the immune system response to help you understand the serious battles going on inside you.

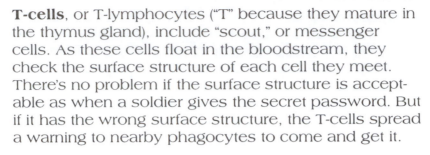

T-cells check the surface structure of cells like a soldier checks for a secret password.

B-cells remember the enemy.

B-cells document antigen patterns.

T-cells give the warning.

The enemy has landed!

NK-cells spew out poison to kill the enemy.

Phagocytes surround the enemy.

# THE IMMUNE AND LYMPH SYSTEMS

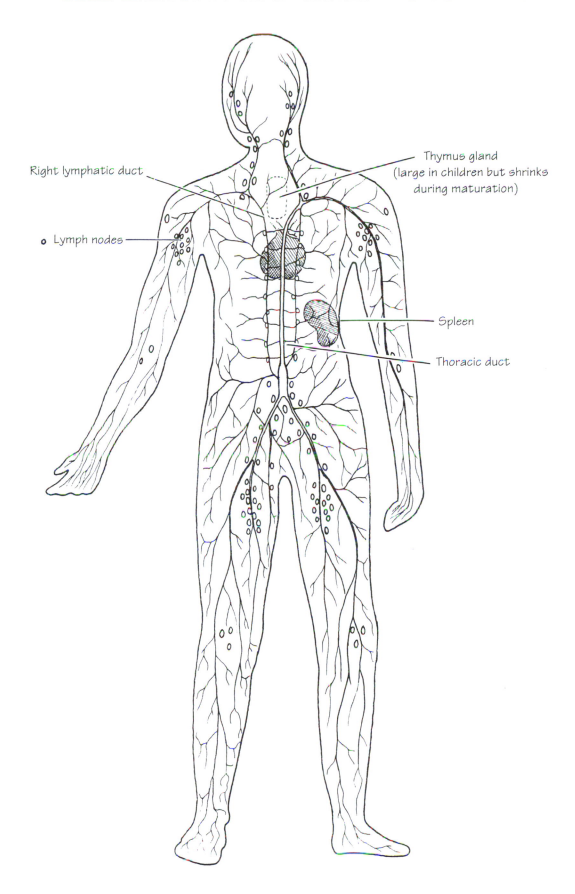

Right lymphatic duct

Lymph nodes

Thymus gland
(large in children but shrinks
during maturation)

Spleen

Thoracic duct

# THE RESPIRATORY SYSTEM

(to the tune of "The Man on the Flying Trapeze")
The melody is from a turn of the century circus song.

Lungs fill up with air with the great - est of
The al - ve - o - li are sacs filled up with

ease. The air - way to lungs makes the pul - mo - nar - y
air they make up the lungs 'cause there's mil - lions right

tree. The trunk is the trach - ea the branch - es bron -
there. And ox - y - gen flows to the blood - stream quite

chi. And the twigs in - to bronch - ioles di - vide.
new ex - changed for the old C - O - 2.

Through the nose or the mouth that join at the phar -

ynx through the tra - che - a past the lar - ynx

the voice box, but air con - tin - ues to bron -

chi, bronchioles to al - ve - o - li.

# THE RESPIRATORY SYSTEM

It's obvious that you need to breathe, but do you know that every one of your trillion-plus cells needs to breathe, too? Just as a fire needs oxygen to burn, your cells also need oxygen to "burn" your food in order to get energy. The cells in your body combine food with oxygen in a process called **respiration**. As cells burn oxygen, like a factory would gas or coal, they give off a waste product called carbon dioxide. The main job of the respiratory system is to bring in oxygen and remove carbon dioxide.

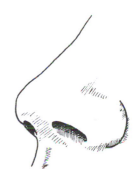

Your cells need fresh air. Cells "breathe" oxygen and expel carbon dioxide.

Tissues and organs from other body systems are needed to complete the transfer of oxygen to your cells, and to pick up carbon dioxide from your cells. For example, the circulatory system removes carbon dioxide by transferring it to capillaries when they deliver fresh oxygen . But the means by which the oxygen comes into your body is through the respiratory system. In order for oxygen to reach cells, it first must pass through the system's specific parts:

1-**nose** which connects to the...
2-**pharynx** which includes the...
3-**larynx** which leads to the...
4-**trachea** which branches into two...
5-**bronchi** which branch into smaller and smaller...
6-**bronchioles** which end in...
7-**alveoli** which collectively make up...
8-**lungs**

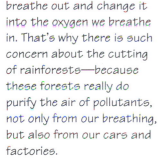

A forest is an oxygen farm! Trees and other plants use the carbon dioxide we breathe out and change it into the oxygen we breathe in. That's why there is such concern about the cutting of rainforests—because these forests really do purify the air of pollutants, not only from our breathing, but also from our cars and factories.

## NOSE
Although your nose contains nerve endings for your sense of smell, it is also a major entry—the best entry—for oxygen. Your nose screens air impurities with hair and mucous membrane and moistens and warms the air to the right temperature for your body.

## PHARYNX
The nose and mouth meet at a chamber located behind them called the **pharynx**, part of your throat area. It leads to two passageways: one for food, called the esophagus; and the other for air. Just below is a leaf-like structure called the **epiglottis** which works like a trapdoor

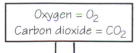

Oxygen = $O_2$
Carbon dioxide = $CO_2$

Nose
The area just inside your nostrils is called the vestibule.

over the **larynx**, keeping food out of air passageways. The larynx is the **voice box** containing **vocal cords** that vibrate with air currents as you make sounds. You can feel and sometimes see the larynx in the front of your neck—it's the "Adam's apple."

### THE PULMONARY TREE

Air passageways in your respiratory system are called the pulmonary tree because they look like an up-side-down tree as they branch into smaller "twigs" inside your lungs. These passageways include your **trachea**, **bronchi**, and **bronchioles**. They all produce mucus and have hair-like cilia to keep out dirt and unwanted particles.

Your trachea, or windpipe, is a four-inch passageway from your throat to the upper-chest. It's strengthened by horse shoe-shaped cartilage that encircles it. The trachea branches into two bronchi leading into the two lungs. The bronchi are also reinforced with cartilage. The bronchi branch into bronchioles, which subdivide into smaller and smaller ones. Bronchioles have smooth muscle for support but do not have cartilage.

The pulmonary tree: The trachea is the trunk, the bronchi are branches, and the bronchioles are twigs.

### ALVEOLI

Alveoli—300 million of them—are clusters of air sacs at the end of bronchioles. The sac walls are only a single cell thick but the outer surface is covered with capillaries to allow the easy transfer of carbon dioxide and oxygen. The fresh oxygen you breathe when you inhale passes through the alveoli and enters the blood-stream at the capillaries. The process works in reverse as carbon dioxide is transferred to alveoli from the capillaries and expelled from your body when you exhale.

Alveoli covered with capillaries.

### LUNGS

You have two spongy lungs made up of alveoli. The right one has three lobes, or parts, and the smaller left (to make room for your heart) has two. Lungs are covered with a slippery membrane called a **pleura** to protect them and allow them to slide against the heart and chest cavity. Lungs filter the air, catching any impurities that have slipped by the air passageways.

Capillaries exchange oxygen for carbon dioxide at alveoli.

If you lightly touch your larynx in the front of your neck as you sing, you can feel the lifting and falling of the larynx to make high and low notes.

# THE RESPIRATORY SYSTEM

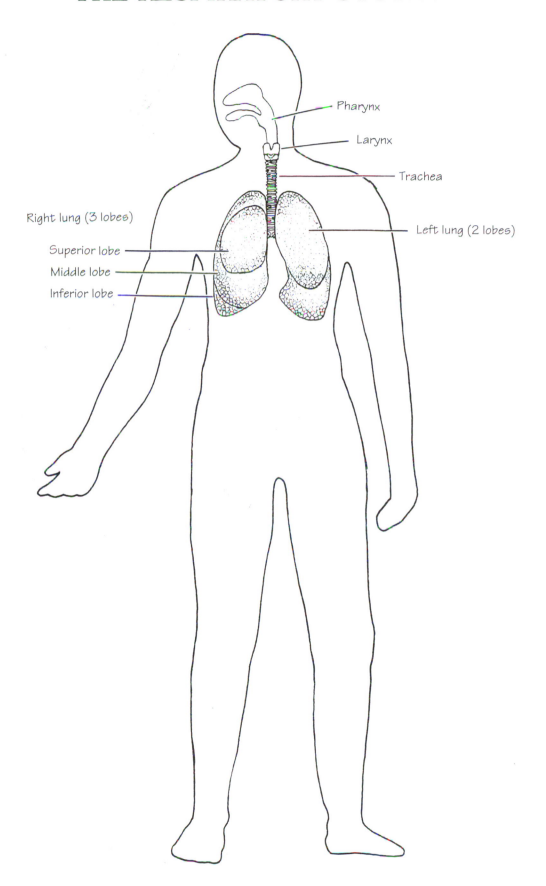

Pharynx

Larynx

Trachea

Right lung (3 lobes)

Left lung (2 lobes)

Superior lobe

Middle lobe

Inferior lobe

# THE ENDOCRINE SYSTEM

(to the tune of "Fox went out on a Chilly Night")
Here's a melody from an old folk song about a fox and the trouble
he causes a farmer.

Duct - less glands that are with - in they are called the en - do - crine make

chem - i - cals that flow with - in and work with the ner - vous sys - tem.

Hor - mones, hor - mones chem - i - cal mes - sen - gers are

what we call the hor - mones.

Each gland produces one-or-more hormones
With names that end with "...ins" and "...ones"
Cortisone, testosterone
Are just two of the hormones
Hormones, hormones
Estrogen, progesterone are two more of the hormones

Adrenal makes adrenaline
Fight or flight that comes from them
Pancreas makes insulin
Milk begins with prolactin
Hormones, hormones
The quantity is so tiny but you need all your hormones

Thyroid and the ovaries
Pituitary and the testes
All the glands they do secrete
Directly in the bloodstream
Hormones, hormones
Stimulate body functions: the duty of your hormones

# THE ENDOCRINE SYSTEM

*Did you say "duckless"? I'm rather fond of my ducks and I wouldn't want to be without them!*

Your body has two kinds of glands: **exocrine** which means "outside," and **endocrine** which means "inside." Exocrine glands **secrete** (release) their chemicals into **ducts** (tubes) that carry them outside your body. For example, sweat glands secrete perspiration (sweat). Exocrine glands also secrete chemicals into ducts that flow into body cavities. For example, salivary glands release saliva into your mouth.

## HORMONES

The endocrine glands empty their chemicals, **hormones**, directly into blood vessels to be carried throughout your body. Hormones are chemical messengers that stimulate other activities and processes. Sex hormones, for example, cause boys and girls to develop to sexual maturity, but other hormones control lifelong activities like digestion, production of urine, and even the preparation of your body to respond to emergencies.

The endocrine system is very complex, and researchers are constantly discovering new influences that hormones have on our bodies. Hormones can make things happen quickly, as in times of fright, or slowly, as in physical growth. Hormones may also work together in a seesaw fashion: one hormone can stimulate the production of another, while an entirely different hormone can suppress its production.

*Well, I said "ductless." You don't need any ducts (or little tubes) to carry hormones where they need to go because the bloodstream does the job. So... You can keep your ducks*

## ENDOCRINE GLANDS

Nine major endocrine glands create nearly 100 hormones. They are scattered throughout the brain and trunk of the body, but are always located next to blood vessels. Endocrine glands include:

1-**hypothalamus**
2-**pituitary**
3-**pineal**
4-**thyroid**
5-**parathyroid**
6-**thymus**
7-**adrenal**
8-**pancreas**
9-**testes or ovaries**

In addition to the endocrine glands, several organs make hormones: the liver, kidneys, stomach, intestines and even the heart.

1-The **hypothalamus**, at the top of the brain stem, coordinates the brain and nervous system with the endocrine system. As mentioned previously, the hypothalamus controls body temperature, thirst and hunger. For purposes of the endocrine system, it controls the pituitary gland. It's the link between the brain and pituitary gland.

**2-**The **pituitary gland** is only about the size of a pea but it is considered perhaps the most important gland. It regulates other glands because it produces hormones that stimulate other glands to release their hormones. For example, during adolescence, the pituitary gland releases hormones that cause the sex glands (testes in boys and ovaries in girls) to release hormones for sexual development. The pituitary gland also produces several other hormones, including **somatotropin** for the development of bones and muscles.

The pineal and pituitary gland signal to the rest of the body that it's time to grow up.

**3-**The **pineal gland** works with the pituitary gland to signal to the rest of the body that it's time to grow up and become sexually mature. It also secretes **serotonin** and **melatonin**. Serotonin promotes a feeling of well-being and melatonin helps you sleep. Melatonin production is affected by the amount of daylight; it increases when it's dark and ceases when it's light.

**4-**The **thyroid** controls body development and **metabolism**, the rate fuel is used in your body.

**5-**The **parathyroid glands**, behind the thyroid, secrete parathormone, which moves calcium from the bones to the blood.

**6-**The **thymus** stimulates the production of white blood cells.

**7-**The **adrenal glands** make the "fight or flight" hormone, **adrenaline**, or **adrenalin**, when you are frightened, alarmed, afraid or excited. Your heartbeat and breathing speed up, and your body tenses, as blood is sent to your arms and legs to get you ready to stand your ground to fight, or to run away.

**8-**The **pancreas** is both an exocrine gland secreting enzymes during digestion, and an endocrine gland secreting **insulin** for controlling the level of sugar in the blood after a meal. Endocrine activity occurs in the **islets of Langerhans**, 200,000 to 1,800,000 cell clusters scattered throughout the pancreas.

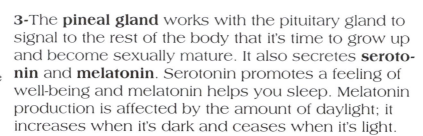

Hey. I hear you all don't have any ducts!

**9-**The **testes** produce male hormones, called **androgens**, including **testosterone**. **Ovaries** produce the female hormones **estrogen** and **progesterone**.

# THE ENDOCRINE SYSTEM

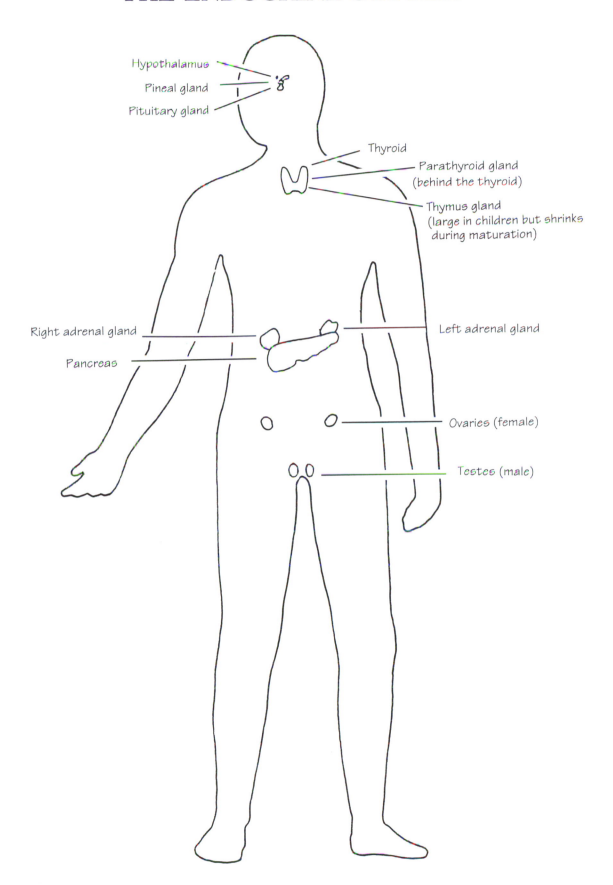

Hypothalamus

Pineal gland

Pituitary gland

Thyroid

Parathyroid gland
(behind the thyroid)

Thymus gland
(large in children but shrinks
during maturation)

Right adrenal gland

Pancreas

Left adrenal gland

Ovaries (female)

Testes (male)

# *"OLOGIES"* (THE STUDY OF)

(to the tune of "Jamaica Farewell")

Calypso, a catchy, rhythmic sound from the Caribbean Islands, was popularized in the United States during the 1950s. Here's the melody from a favorite, traditional folk song of Jamaica.

# *"OLOGIES"* (THE STUDY OF)

The study of the human body is divided into many specific areas. When you see a word ending in *ology*, it means the study of whatever the first part of the word means. Many scientific words are like word puzzles, fitting together Greek or Latin root words with different prefixes and suffixes. The word "psychology" is a good example: *psych* means "the mind" and *ology* means "the study of." So the definition of psychology is the study of the mind, behavior and mental processes.

Some especially long words combine several root words such as in otorhinolaryngology:

> *oto* means eye
> *rhino* means nose
> *laryng* means larynx or throat
> *ology* means the study of

Maybe you have never heard of a otorhinolaryngologist? Instead, these specialists call themselves ear, nose and throat doctors.

The suffix *ology* is the main ending for any area of science, such as biology (the study of life)—or even non-science, such as the disproven phrenology (the study of head bumps). There are a few exceptions to *ology* as a word ending. A major study of the human body is "anatomy," which means "the study of structures" (i.e. the skeleton); another exception is *try*, as in dentistry and psychiatry.

## BRANCHES OF SCIENCE

Many branches of medical science can be classified as a study of a particular organ or organ system of the body. Other fields such as parasitology (the study of parasites) or virology (the study of viruses) involve the human body in that scientists research the diseases the micro-organisms cause. Listed on the next page are body systems and some of the terminology (the study of terms) associated with them. You'll notice that many of the root words look similar to terms in this book. You have become familiar with words such as "cardiac," so you already have a good idea what "cardiology" means.

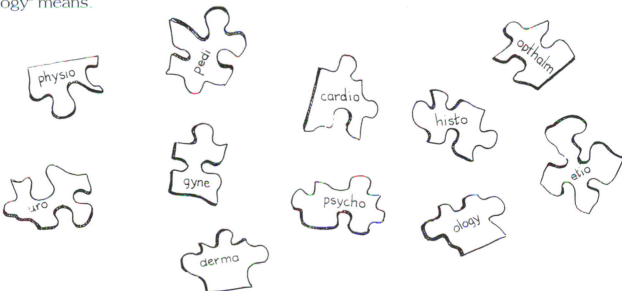

Don't let scientific words confuse you. They are made of root words scientists put together like puzzles—like word puzzles.

### Circulatory System

cardiology:
The study of the heart and vascular (vessels) system.

> *cardio* means "heart"

hemotology or hematology:
The study of blood and blood-forming tissues.

> *hemo* or *hema* means "blood"

### Digestive System

gastroenterology:
The study of the digestive system including the functions and disorders of the stomach, intestines, pancreas, and liver.

> *gastro* means "stomach" or "belly"
> *entero* means "intestines"

### Endocrine System

endocrinology:
The study of the glands and hormones of the endocrine system.

> *endo* means "within"
> *crine* or *krin* means "to separate"

neuroendocrinology:
The study of the interactions between the nervous and endocrine systems.

> *neuro* means "nerve"
> *endo* means "within"
> *crine* means "to separate"

### Excretory System

urology:
The study of the urinary tract and its diseases; also the study of the male reproductive system.

> *uro* means "urine" or "urinary tract," (same root as in ureter, urethra)

### Immune System

immunohematology:
The study of the immune systems involving blood (as in blood banking)

> *immune* means "exempt"
> *hemo* means "blood"

immunology:
The study of the body's defense system

> *immune* means "exempt" or "being resistant to a pathogen"

psychoneuroimmunology:
The study of the relationship of the mind and nervous system with the immune system.

> *psycho* means "the mind"
> *neuro* means "nerve"
> *immuno* means "exempt" or "being resistant to a pathogen"

### Muscular System

physiology:
The study of normal functions of the body and its chemical and physical methods.

> *physio* means "nature" or "natural function" (same root as in physician, physical)

### Nervous System

electrophysiology:
The study of electrical processes, as in the heart and brain.

> *electro* means "dealing with electricity"
> *physio* means "natural function"

neurology:
The study of the brain and its diseases.

> *neuro* means "nerve"

psychiatry:
The study of and treatment of mental and emotional disorders.

> *psycho* means "the mind"

psychopathology:
The study of mental disorders.

> *psycho* means "the mind"
> *patho* means "suffering"

### Reproductive System

embryology:
The study of development from a seed or egg to the established form or shape.

> *em* means "to be full of, to swell"

fetology:
The study of the fetus, as distinguished from the study of the embryo.

> *fetus* means "pregnant"

gynecology:
The study of the female reproductive system.

> *gyne* means "woman, female"

neonatology:
The study and treatment of the newborn.
> *neo* means "new" or "youthful"
> *natus* means "born"

tocology:
The study of childbirth.
> *tokos* means "childbirth"

## Respiratory System
pulmonology:
The study of the lungs.
> *pulmo* means "lung"

## Sensory System
audiology:
The study of the ear, hearing and balance.
> *audio* means "hearing"

dermatology:
The study of the skin.
> *derma* means "skin"

opthalmology:
The study of anatomy, physiology and diseases of the eye.
> *opthalm* means "eye"

## Skeletal System
anatomy:
The study of the structural organization of the human body.
> *ana* means "to cut up, to dissect."

orthopedics:
The study of the bones, joints and functions of the musculoskeletal system (which develop during childhood).
> *ortho* means "straight, erect"
> *pedi* means "child"

---

The following *ologies* do not easily classify into specific systems but deal with important aspects of the human body.

cytology:
The study of cells.
> *cyto* means "cell"

epidemiology:
The study of disease on populations.
> *epi* means "upon"
> *demos* means "people"
> (same root as in epidemic)

etiology:
The study of the causes of diseases.
> *etio* means "cause"

gerontology:
The study of the care, health and disease of older persons.
> *gero* means "old age"

histology:
The study of form and structure of tissues.
> *histo* means "tissue"

mycology:
The study of fungi.
> *myco* means "mushroom, fungus"

oncology:
The study of cancer or tumors.
> *onco* means "tumor, mass, bulk"

pathology:
The cause, development and effects of disease.
> *patho* means "suffering"

pedology or pediatrics:
The study of disorders and normal physical and mental development of children and young adolescents.
> *pedo* and *pedi* mean "child"

podiatry:
The study of the foot: its anatomy, mechanics and pathology.
> *podo* means "foot"

rheumatology:
The study of diseases that have to do with muscles and joints, such as arthritis.
> *rheuma* means "a flow, stream, or flux." (A flow or discharge of mucus was thought to be the cause of pain in joints.)

toxicology:
The study of poisons
> *toxin* means "poison"

Reference:
*Churchill's Medical Dictionary*. New York: Churchill Livingstone, 1989.

# APPENDIX

# Introduction to the Human Body

(to the tune of "The Rebel Soldier")
Lyrics by Dorry Eldon

Cells that work together in your body form tissues
Tissues form the organs, organs form systems in you
These systems work together to keep your body alive
The nervous system makes them all react so you survive
These systems are keeping you alive

Respiratory system uses oxygen you breathe
In circulatory blood is pumping by heart beat
Some waste is excreted through the urinary tract
Hormones come from endocrine and immune will attack
These systems are keeping you alive

Our bodies they are different for reproductive means
Digest for food absorption but we eat too much it seems
The skeletal connects the bones by the ligaments
The muscular like levers all, control the bone movements
These systems are keeping you alive

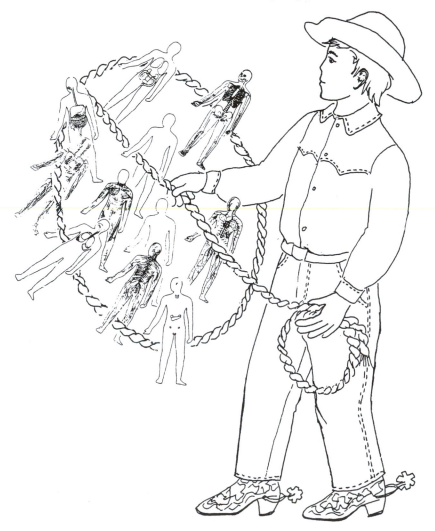

# The Skeletal System

(to the tune of "Tarantella")
Lyrics by Dorry Eldon

Part A: Oh, shiver me timbers don't you know these bones are skeletal
The appendicular skeleton, the other's axial
One is the pelvis, arms and legs, appendages all
The other on the axis are the ribs, spine and the skull

Part B: In my legs are the fibula also the tibia
Femur's the bone in my thigh
The ankle bone tarsals, and the metatarsals
stubbed phalanges make me cry

In my arm is the radius, ulna, and humerus
next to the biceps so strong
In my wrist there are carpals, and the metacarpals
finger phalanges are long

Part C: You have your long bones and your short bones and the flat and irregular
Ligaments join them at the joints, tendons connecting them to muscular
Layers of bones include hard compact and the spongy cancellous too
And there's the marrow in the cavity to make blood cells for all parts of you

Part A: You have two hundred and six bones they all have their own name
But they all connect together to give you the upright frame
With muscles that can move them like levers that you see
But please do not break them or in a cast you will then be

Part B: In my skull there's the frontal, and cavity orbital
And with my mandible chew
They are part of the axial not so the clavicle
but sternum and the ribs too

Oh, the spine with the lumbar, thoracic, and cervical
Sacrum they're all in your back
Connect to the pelvis the hip bone for Elvis
But drink your milk so it won't crack

Part C: You have your long bones and your short bones and the flat and irregular
Ligaments join them at the joints, tendons connecting them to muscular
Layers of bones include hard compact and the spongy cancellous too
And there's the marrow in the cavity to make blood cells for all parts of you

# The Muscular System

(to the tune of "Erie Canal")
Lyrics by Dorry Eldon

Muscles of three types you'll find
Skeletal, smooth, and the cardiac kind
Skeletal muscles come in pairs
With the bones you'll find them there

Workin' together to make you strong
One gets short while the other long
Like your arm when muscles flex
Biceps short and long triceps

Chorus:
Your heart is a muscle too
Skeletal type working like a smooth
A specialized muscle called the cardiac
But your skeletal muscles go right up your back
If you've ever navigated on the Erie Canal

Voluntary muscles all
Striated, the skeletal
Tendons at the bones connect
With the joints so they can flex

Involuntary are the kind
That move with no choice from your mind
Like your stomach with muscles smooth
And in the walls of blood vessels too

Chorus

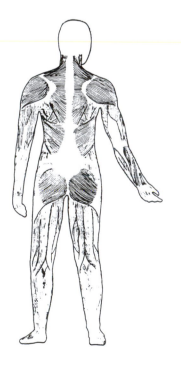
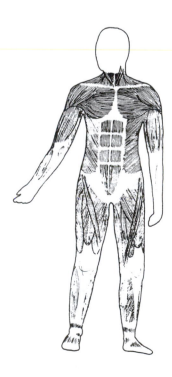

# The Nervous System
(to the tune of "Old Joe Clark")
Lyrics by Dorry Eldon

Nervous system's made up of two,
nerves are the peripheral
Brain and also spinal cord—
they make up the central
Sensory and motor nerves
are in the peripheral
Twelve are called the cranial
thirty-one are spinal

Chorus:
Sending currents from your brain
What your body's needing
To muscles, organs, senses, skin,
Even helps your breathing

Forebrain's hypothalamus and
thalamus and cerebrum
Hindbrain has medulla and
pons and cerebellum
Forebrain is for conscious thought
mid- and hind- make brain stem
With the nerves and spinal cord
for communication

Chorus

Fibers in the cells are the
dendrites and the axons
Covered with a myelin sheath
help the current pass on
Jumping gaps at the synapse
dendrite from the axon
With nucleus, cell bodies are
all part of your neuron

Chorus

Doesn't even use the brain
the system autonomic
Messages to innards are
Rather automatic
Changes when you're angry are
from the sympathetic
Changes when you're calming down
from parasympathetic

Chorus

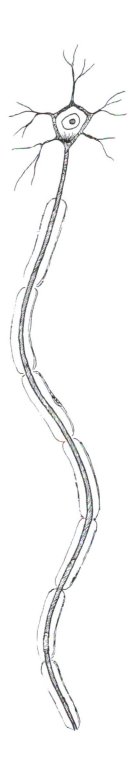

# The Sensory System

(to the tune of "Caissons go Rolling Along")
Lyrics by Dorry Eldon

Ear's divided in three
Auricle the part you see
Middle ear has three little bones
Cochlea's like a shell,
With semicircular canal
Inner ear so you hear all the tones

Chorus:
Organs specialize
To receive the stimuli
To brain by nerves they take it in
Senses number five
Smell, taste, hearing, and your sight
Also touch with the nerves in your skin

Taste buds for food you eat
Bitter, sour, salt or sweet
Papilla and with smell through your nose
With olfactory nerve
Smells the food your momma serves
Three conchae, sinus, and nasal fold

Chorus

Outer eye sclera
On the front it's cornea
Choroid middle of eye layers three
Ciliary to lens
Pupils to let the light in
Optic nerve, retina so you see

Chorus

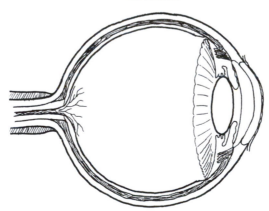

# The Reproductive System
(to the tune of "Star of the County Down")
Lyrics by Dorry Eldon

Oh, the male is able to fertilize the egg
in the female's body within
When the male gives his seed to help create a life,
then a new little babe may begin

Chorus:
For life is a mystery that we live
And our bodies produce life to give
Our genes and our dreams to the children yet unborn
To continue life's cycle again

In the female's body her reproductive system
makes eggs in her ovaries within
In her womb, called the uterus the egg becomes a baby,
when this egg unites with a sperm

Chorus

Egg uniting with sperm is called fertilization
nurtured in mother's womb warm within
Embryo, then a fetus, and then a little babe
is born nine months at full gestation

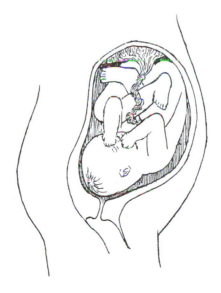

# The Digestive System

(to the tune of "The Coffee in the Army")
Lyrics by Dorry Eldon

In your mouth there is saliva, it's a digestive juice
It mixes as you're eating with particles you chew
Then food will travel down a narrow tube
Called your esophagus,
Continues the process
In the digestion of food

Oh, the stomach has a pear shape, the size of your two fists
The walls are made of muscle, creating peristalsis
There's pepsin, hydrochloric acid, too
Gastric juice makes the chyme
Within five hours' time
In the digestion of food

And in the small intestine, there's pancreatic juice
The liver makes the bile, intestine makes more juice
For food to be absorbed and used as fuel
It passes through the villi
Cells it will satisfy
Cells need digestion of food

And in the large intestine, there's feces as it's called
The waste then leaves your body,
And now you've heard it all
The four main parts for total digestion
Mouth and small intestine
Stomach, large intestine
For the digestion of food

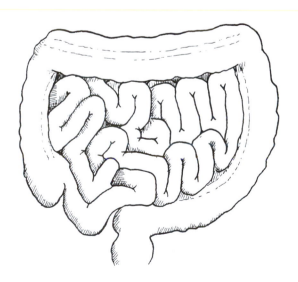

# The Excretory System

(to the tune of "Goober Peas")
Lyrics by Dorry Eldon

Excretion rids the cell waste, it's processes within
But there is perspiration, that's excretion through your skin
Kidneys make the urine, lungs rid $CO_2$
Intestines add some cell waste to the food inside of you

Chorus:
Clean, clean, clean, clean
Your body likes it clean
It has a special system
Just to keep it clean

In the urinary system, kidneys make blood clean
Nephrons purify, it like a filter they will screen
Water from the waste so it can be absorbed
But waste goes to the ureter in the bladder it is stored

Chorus

Urine from the kidneys through ureter it goes
Collecting in the bladder then through urethra flows
Urea is a waste from proteins breaking down
With $CO_2$, ammonia, in urine will be found

Chorus

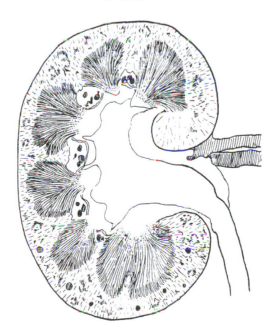

# The Circulatory System

(to the tune of "Red River Valley")
Lyrics by Dorry Eldon

Oh, the bloodstream is a transportation system
Carries food, oxygen, and cell waste
Like small rivers flowing all throughout the body
For the different kinds of cells in every place

Hemoglobin carries such precious cargo
It takes oxygen from lungs to the cells
Then it carries away carbon dioxide
And this waste at the lungs it expels

Oh, the heart keeps a beat to keep blood flowing
Away from the heart in arteries
And the blood flows back to the heart in the veins
And they are connected by capillaries

Oh, the heart is made up of four chambers
The two large ones are called ventricles
At their top the valves are working like a trapdoor
Controlling flow from the two small auricles

Altogether it's the circulatory system
Pulmonary and systemic; there are two
Pulmonary to the lungs, it shortly travels
But systemic goes to all the parts of you

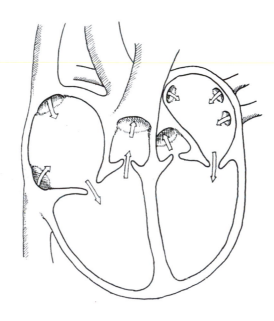

# The Immune and Lymph Systems

(to the tune of "La Cucaracha")
Lyrics by Dorry Eldon

Chorus:
Immune system, with your lymph system
will your enemies attack
With the white blood cells, the leukocyte cells
that will destroy and turn them back

A germ is like a cucaracha
that would love to live inside ya
But white blood cells just won't allow it
and when discovered will destroy it

Bacteria or germs, pester
Like with splinters when they fester
Your body calls on the white blood cells
just to help you in those sick spells

Chorus

There's several kinds of the white blood cells
Phagocyte with macrophage cells
Their enemies they love to eat 'em
Wherever they hunt as they meet 'em

The lymphocytes include the T-cells
Messengers to all the B-cells
B-cells can make the antibodies
That match and remember germ armies

Chorus

The lymph is watery fluid
With white blood cells in a liquid
Bathing tissues, then as it flows
Gets purified in all the lymph nodes

Lymph system is a sewer system
For all the tissues cause it cleans 'em
It moves the waste into lymph vessels
That move with no pump but with muscles

Chorus

# The Respiratory System

(to the tune of "The Man on the Flying Trapeze")
Lyrics by Dorry Eldon

Lungs fill up with air, with the greatest of ease
The airway to lungs makes the pulmonary tree
The trunk is the trachea, the branches, bronchi
And the twigs into bronchioles divide

Chorus:
Through the nose or the mouth that join at the pharynx
Through the trachea past the larynx,
The voice box, but air continues to bronchi,
bronchioles to alveoli

The alveoli are sacs filled up with air
They make up the lungs 'cause there's millions right there
And oxygen flows to the bloodstream quite new
Exchanged for the old $CO_2$

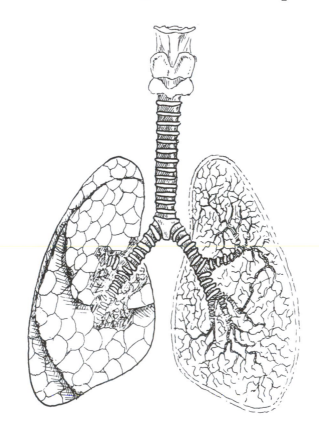

# The Endocrine System

(to the tune of "Fox went out on a Chilly Night")
Lyrics by Dorry Eldon

Ductless glands that are within
They are called the endocrine
Make chemicals that flow within; and work with the nervous system
Hormones, hormones
Chemical messengers are what you call the hormones

Each gland produces one or more hormones
With names that end with "...ins" and "...ones"
Cortisone, testosterone are just two of the hormones
Hormones, hormones
Estrogen, progesterone are two more of the hormones

Adrenal makes adrenaline
Fight or flight that comes from them
Pancreas makes insulin
Milk begins with prolactin
Hormones, hormones
The quantity is so tiny but you need all your hormones

Thyroid and the ovaries
Pituitary and the testes
All the glands they do secrete directly in the bloodstream
Hormones, hormones
Stimulate body functions: the duty of your hormones

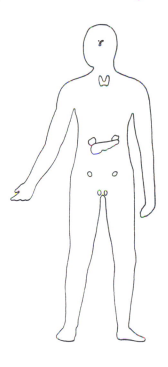

# "Ologies" (the study of)
(to the tune of "Jamaica Farewell")
Lyrics by Dorry Eldon

"The study of" is called an "ology" you can find it often at the end of words
As life science called biology which of course is the study of all living things

Chorus:
Oh the study of tissues: histology
Actions of your body: physiology
The study of cells is cytology
And the study of the blood is hemotology

The science of human biology is divided into subjects and is specialized
To help scientists understand and to study and the doctors medicines prescribe

Chorus 2:
The study of the eyes is opthomology
Study of the heart is cardiology
The study of the brain is called neurology
And the study of the skin is dermatology

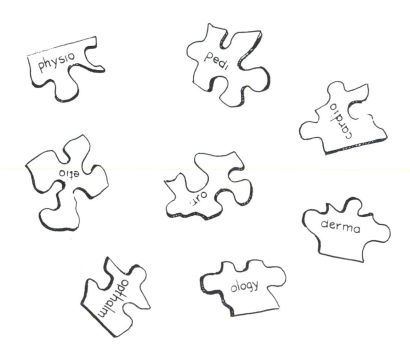

# BIBLIOGRAPHY

Allison, Linda. *Blood and Guts*. New York: Scholastic Inc., 1977.

Ballar, Carol. *The Heart and Circulatory System*. Texas: Raintree Steck–Vaughn, 1997.

*Churchill's Medical Dictionary,* New York Churchill Livingstone, 1989.

Day, Trevor. *The Random House Book of 1001 Questions and Answers about The Human Body*. New York: Random House, 1994.

Edelson, Edward. *The Nervous System*. New York: Chelsea House Publications, 1991.

Engel-Arieli, Susan L. M.D. *How Your Body Works*. Emeryville, CA: Ziff-Davis Press, 1994.

Feinberg, Brian. *The Musculoskeletal System*. New York: Chelsea House Publishers, 1993.

Kalina, Sigmund. *Your Blood and Its Cargo*. New York: Lothrop Lee and Shepard Co., 1974.

Knight, David C. *Your Body's Defenses*. New York: McGraw-Hill, 1975.

National Geographic Society. Washington D.C.: *The Incredible Machine,* 1986.

Nourse, Alan. *Your Immune System*. New York: Franklin Watts,1982.

Schuman, Benjamin N. Atheneum, New York: *The Human Skeleton* , 1965.

Silverstein, Alvin, Virginia, and Robert. *Circulatory Systems: The Rivers Within*. Englewood Cliffs, New Jersey: Prentice-Hall, Inc., 1970.

Silverstein, Alvin, Virginia, and Robert. *The Digestive System*. New York: Twenty-First Century Books, 1994.

Silverstein, Alvin, Virginia, and Robert. *The Muscular System*. New York: Twenty-First Century Books, 1994.

Silverstein, Alvin, Virginia, and Robert. *The Nervous System*. New York: Twenty-First Century Books, 1994.

Silverstein, Alvin, Virginia, and Robert. *The Skeletal System*. New York: Twenty-First Century Books, 1994.

Ward, Brian. *Food and Digestion*. London: Franklin Watts, 1983.

Zim, Herbert M. *Bones*. New York: William Morrow and Company, 1969.

# INDEX